Fourth and long, and the clock is ticking: Who's the Giants' all-time interception champ?

Which team won Super Bowl IX on January 12, 1975?

What is John Elway's middle name: Albert, Eugene, Morris, or Nathan?

Name any one of the six players whose numbers have been retired by the Detroit Lions.

Who was the AFC rushing leader in 1996?

Name the two players who combined on an NFL-record 104-yard interception return for the Philadelphia Eagles in a 1996 defeat of the Dallas Cowboys.

Rush for short yardage or take to the air for the bomb: how you do depends on what you know!

THE PRO FOOTBALL TRIVIA BOWL

THE PRO FOOTBALL
TRIVIA BOWL

STEVE GREENBERG

AVON BOOKS ◆ NEW YORK

AVON BOOKS, INC.
1350 Avenue of the Americas
New York, New York 10019

Copyright © 1998 by Steve Greenberg
Published by arrangement with the author
Library of Congress Catalog Card Number: 98-93298
ISBN: 0-380-79946-4
www.avonbooks.com

First Avon Books Printing: December 1998

AVON TRADEMARK REG. U.S. PAT. OFF. AND IN OTHER COUNTRIES, MARCA
REGISTRADA, HECHO EN U.S.A.

Printed in the U.S.A.

WCD 10 9 8 7 6 5 4 3 2

To my "Quiz Book Widow"

CONTENTS

Contents

Answers follow each chapter

INTRODUCTION

We sports trivia buffs are a misunderstood breed. To those without the gift for soaking up names and numbers, socking them away, and trotting them out for timeless use, we are, at the very least, a little goofy, and maybe even in need of a life.

Of course, we know better. Those on the outside may not believe it, but we don't spend our days inhaling statistics, scouring old box scores, and rewinding game tapes. No, we watch a ball game, we read a game story, we see a list of all-time leaders, and the stuff just sticks to us like glue.

Who's the NFL's all-time leading rusher? Shoot, don't insult us. Who stands *eighth* on the list? Now you're talking. Seen it once, and once was enough.

Some might snicker and ask, "Why, then, if you aren't merely a gaggle of wannabe jocks, do you spend endless hours creating books like this one?"

Well, that's a tough one to answer. The joy of knowing so much about a sport such as pro football, after all, isn't in researching its history and recording the findings on paper. It's the way it takes you back. It's the way it helps create friendships. It's the way it keeps the more important details of life from consuming you.

Perhaps the best answer is that a book such as this one

keeps the chain moving. Someone, somewhere, will be kind enough to give it a good read, and eventually he'll be amazed at all he remembers.

THE PLAYBOOK

The Pro Football Trivia Bowl is much more than a book of NFL-related questions and answers. It's a *football game,* only without the cracked ribs and spindly hamstrings. There are runs and passes, field goals and punts. There is defense, if the players so choose. There is all the strategy of the real thing.

Questions are chosen from the following categories, with each category having its own yardage value: Quarterback Sneaks (one yard), Clouds of Dust (three yards), Quick Outs (five yards), Tight End Curls (seven yards), Gaping Holes (10 yards), Crossing Routes (15 yards), Post Patterns (20 yards), Breakaway Runs (30 yards), and Bombs Away (50 yards). There are also Field Goals (inside 20 yards, 20–29 yards, 30–39 yards, 40–49 yards, and 50–55 yards) and Two-Point Conversions. Naturally, the questions become more difficult as the yardage value or field-goal distance increases.

Each player's playbook includes 25 Quarterback Sneaks, 100 Clouds of Dust, 75 Quick Outs, 50 Tight End Curls, 50 Gaping Holes, 50 Crossing Routes, 50 Post Patterns, 25 Breakaway Runs, and 25 Bombs Away. Each playbook also includes 25 questions for each Field-Goal distance, and 25 Two-Point Conversions.

THE RULES

Players flip a coin to determine who has the choice to begin on offense or defense; the player who begins the game on offense does so at his own 20-yard line. He calls plays by calling the name of a play category (such as Clouds of Dust) on each down; which question is asked is up to his opponent—that's how defense is played. (However, players might find it preferable for the offensive player to randomly choose a question number, or they might agree to ask the questions within each category in order.) Of course, players are on their honor to notify their opponents if a particular question already has been answered.

Moving the ball. Just like in the NFL, the player on offense must advance 10 yards in four downs—four questions or fewer to earn a fresh set of downs. Whenever a player reaches fourth down, he has three options: He can punt (all punts travel 40 yards, with no returns; those snapped from within the opponent's 40-yard line give the opponent first-and-10 at his own goal line); he can kick a field goal (all made field goals are worth three points; the length of all field goal attempts, as in the NFL, can be determined by adding 17 yards to the line of scrimmage); or he can "go for it." If he goes for the first down and fails to convert, his opponent takes possession at the yard line where the play ended.

When a player scores a touchdown (worth six points), he can either accept an automatic seventh point or attempt a two-point conversion. Afterward, the opponent takes possession at his 20-yard line.

Game length. Game length can be addressed in any manner the players choose. One possibility is for regulation to end as soon as the players have combined for 20 possessions; after a total of five possessions, the first quarter ends, five more brings an end to the first half, and so on.

A second option for ''keeping time'' is to do just that: keep time. Players can, for instance, decide to play for a total of two hours (or 30 minutes a quarter), with a running clock that stops only for bathroom breaks, sandwich breaks, knocks at the front door, etc. In this scenario, the offensive player calls a play right away after the previous play's yardage is accounted for; once the play is called, the defensive player must ask a question in 30 seconds or less, and then the offensive player has up to 30 seconds to answer the question. With a time clock in effect, timeouts (three a half for each team) must be included so that, for example, a defensive player can't let the clock run out in order to stop a potential game-winning field goal.

And, of course, players have the option of shortening or extending the game to as many possessions or as much time as they choose.

Ties. Finally, in the event of a tie at the end of regulation, the game—no matter how it is being timed—moves into sudden-death overtime, meaning the first score (touchdown or field goal) wins. Once again, a coin is flipped to determine which player has the choice to begin on offense or defense, and the player who starts on offense does so from his 20-yard line. If there has been no change in score after a full overtime period (the same length as one quarter), the players must decide whether to end the game in a tie or play on into a second overtime period.

Let's all just hope that, whether you win, lose, or draw, there are plenty of rematches.

PLAYER ONE

QUARTERBACK SNEAKS

(25 questions, one yard each)

1. Name the respective NFL teams Hall of Fame linebackers Dick Butkus and Ray Nitschke played for.
2. By what nickname was Hall of Fame halfback Harold Grange known?
3. If an official makes a grasping motion in front of his face with one hand, what is he signaling?
4. What position do All-Pro offensive linemen Tony Boselli and Willie Roaf play: center, guard, or tackle?
5. With what team did Bill Parcells have his first NFL head coaching job?
6. What team did the Denver Broncos defeat 31–24 in Super Bowl XXXII?
7. How many timeouts is a team allowed each half?
8. With what team did cornerback Rod Woodson play the first 10 seasons of his NFL career (1987–96) before signing as a free agent with the San Francisco 49ers in 1997?
9. How many Super Bowls have the New Orleans Saints won?
10. To what team did the San Francisco 49ers lose the 1996 NFC West title on a tie-breaker?

11. How many yards is an offense penalized for illegal motion?

12. Name the Ohio State offensive tackle the St. Louis Rams selected with the number one overall pick in the 1997 NFL draft.

13. What position do All-Pro defensive linemen Cortez Kennedy and Chester McGlockton play: end or tackle?

14. How many yards is an offense penalized for a delay of game?

15. With what team did quarterback Jim Harbaugh play the first seven seasons of his NFL career (1987–93) before signing as a free agent with the Indianapolis Colts in 1994?

16. If an offensive player carries the ball over the front end of the opposing team's goal line but not over the back end, is it a touchdown?

17. What team did the San Francisco 49ers defeat 55–10 in Super Bowl XXIV?

18. Who is the NFL's all-time rushing leader?

19. How many yards is an offense penalized for holding?

20. Who was the starting quarterback of the Chicago Bears in their championship season of 1985?

21. How many Super Bowls have the Buffalo Bills won?

22. When measuring for a first down, what part of the ball is used: the forward point or the backward point?

23. What position do NFLers Raymont Harris and Harvey Williams play?

24. If an official extends both his arms above his head (without placing his hands together), what is he signaling?

25. What was Hall of Fame defensive tackle Joe Greene's nickname during his playing days with the Pittsburgh Steelers?

ANSWERS

1. Butkus played for the Chicago Bears from 1965 to 1973 and was inducted into the Hall in '79; Nitschke played for the Green Bay Packers from 1958 to 1972 and was inducted in '78.
2. "Red." Grange, who played in 1925 and from 1929 to 1934 with the Chicago Bears, and in 1926 and '27 with the New York Yankees of the AFL, also was known as "the Galloping Ghost."
3. A face-masking penalty.
4. Tackle.
5. The New York Giants, whom Parcells led from 1983 to 1990, winning two Super Bowls along the way.
6. The Green Bay Packers.
7. Three.
8. The Pittsburgh Steelers, with whom he started 125 games, intercepted 38 passes, and played in seven Pro Bowls. He then played one season with the 49ers before signing as a free agent in 1998 with the Baltimore Ravens.
9. None. The Saints never have been to the Super Bowl.
10. The Carolina Panthers. Both teams were 12–4, but the Panthers beat the 49ers both times the teams played that season.
11. Five.
12. Orlando Pace.
13. Tackle.
14. Five.
15. The Chicago Bears, with whom he started 65 games and threw for 11,567 yards and 50 touchdowns.
16. Yes. The goal line actually is part of the end zone;

it's a touchdown if the ball is on, above, or over the goal line.

17. The Denver Broncos.
18. Hall-of-Famer Walter Payton, who rushed for 16,726 yards for the Chicago Bears from 1975 to 1987.
19. Ten.
20. Jim McMahon, who made his only Pro Bowl that season after completing 178 of 313 passes for 2,392 yards and 15 touchdowns, with 11 interceptions.
21. None. The Bills, who did win AFL championships in 1964 and '65, are 0–4 in Super Bowls.
22. The forward point.
23. Running back.
24. A touchdown (or a field goal, or a successful extra-point kick).
25. "Mean Joe."

CLOUDS OF DUST

(100 questions, three yards each)

1. In what facility did the Baltimore Ravens play their home games in 1997?
2. With what NFL team did linebacker Bryan Cox play for five seasons (1991–95) before signing as a free agent with the Chicago Bears in 1996?
3. What team did the Denver Broncos defeat 24–21 on the road in the 1997 AFC Championship Game?
4. What jersey number did Hall of Fame quarterback Terry Bradshaw wear: number 4, number 8, number 12, or number 16?
5. Which one of the following NFLers did *not* play at Notre Dame: Jerome Bettis, Tim Brown, Elvis Grbac, or Rick Mirer?
6. Former Cincinnati Bengals running back Ickey Woods had a touchdown dance that became famous during his team's run to the AFC championship in 1988. What was the dance called?
7. Name the former defensive lineman who is the lone Tampa Bay Buccaneers representative in the Pro Football Hall of Fame.
8. Who won more games (including playoffs) as San Francisco 49ers coach: George Seifert or Bill Walsh?

9. Where did Detroit Lions running back Barry Sanders play in college?

10. What AFC East player in 1996 set the NFL record for pass receptions by a rookie?

11. What is the nickname of NFL defensive tackle James Geathers?

12. Name the former Pittsburgh Steelers (1974–88) and Kansas City Chiefs (1989–90) center who played in nine Pro Bowls and was inducted into the Pro Football Hall of Fame in 1997.

13. New York Jets quarterback Joe Namath guaranteed a victory in Super Bowl III and delivered, leading his team to a 16–7 victory. What team did the Jets defeat?

14. Who led the NFL in rushing in 1996: the Pittsburgh Steelers' Jerome Bettis or the Detroit Lions' Barry Sanders?

15. Defensive tackle Wayne Martin signed a contract extension in 1997 to remain with the same NFC team he'd played for since 1989. Name the team.

16. In what facility did the Denver Broncos play their home games in 1998?

17. Name the defensive tackle who was the Oakland Raiders' first pick (number two overall) in the 1997 NFL draft.

18. Who was the Cincinnati Bengals' coach from 1984 to 1991?

19. In what facility did the Pittsburgh Steelers play their home games in 1998?

20. From the AFL-NFL merger in 1970 through the '97 season, which one of the following teams has a winning record in regular-season interconference play (AFC vs. NFC): the New Orleans Saints or the Oakland (and Los Angeles) Raiders?

21. Which one of the following teams has an all-time winning record on ''Monday Night Football''

(through 1997): the Atlanta Falcons or the San Diego Chargers?

22. Who did Dick Vermeil replace in 1997 as St. Louis Rams coach?

23. Name the former AFC West wide receiver who caught at least one pass in 177 consecutive games, all with the same team. (Hint: He played in the NFL from 1976 to 1989.)

24. Name any one of the four players whose jersey numbers have been retired by the Atlanta Falcons.

25. Name the AFC Central player who led the NFL in rushing in 1978, '79, and '80, and led the AFC in rushing in '81.

26. What jersey number does Detroit Lions running back Barry Sanders wear?

27. Name any two of the five players whose jersey numbers have been retired by the Cleveland Browns.

28. Where did Miami Dolphins quarterback Dan Marino play in college?

29. In what facility did the Chicago Bears play their home games in 1998?

30. What jersey number does Green Bay Packers quarterback Brett Favre wear?

31. What AFC East team finished with a 1–15 record in 1996?

32. After spending his first five NFL seasons with the San Diego Chargers, what AFC team did wide receiver Shawn Jefferson join in 1996?

33. With what NFL team did defensive end Jim Jeffcoat play for the first 12 seasons of his career (1983–94) before signing as a free agent with the Buffalo Bills in 1995?

34. What position did Brent Jones, who was with the San Francisco 49ers from 1987 to 1997, play?

35. What NFL team was coached by Dick MacPherson in 1991 and '92?

36. For what team did Curt Warner rush for 6,705 yards from 1983 to 1989?

37. Name the Chicago Bears quarterback who in 1995 set team single-season records for passing yards (3,838) and touchdown passes (29).

38. What jersey number has running back Jerome Bettis worn throughout his NFL career?

39. In what facility did the Detroit Lions play their home games in 1998?

40. What jersey number does Miami Dolphins quarterback Dan Marino wear?

41. What NFL team did Ron Meyer coach from the fourteenth game of 1986 to the fifth game of '91?

42. From the AFL-NFL merger in 1970 through the '97 season, which one of the following teams has a winning record in regular-season interconference play (AFC vs. NFC): the Arizona (and Phoenix and St. Louis) Cardinals or the Pittsburgh Steelers?

43. Name any two of the seven players whose jersey numbers have been retired by the Indianapolis (formerly Baltimore) Colts.

44. Who has been the NFL commissioner since 1989?

45. Name any one of the four players whose jersey numbers have been retired by the Tennessee (formerly Houston) Oilers.

46. What team won Super Bowl XXIX on January 29, 1995?

47. With what team did wide receiver Don Beebe play the first six seasons of his NFL career (1989–94)?

48. With what team did safety Bennie Blades play the first nine seasons of his NFL career (1988–96) before signing as a free agent in 1997 with the Seattle Seahawks?

49. Name any two of the four players whose jersey numbers have been retired by the Green Bay Packers.

50. In what facility did the Minnesota Vikings play their home games in 1998?

51. Name the last AFC team to win the Super Bowl.

52. Before taking over the Dallas Cowboys in 1994, Barry Switzer's only previous head coaching job came at what university?

53. Which one of the following teams has an all-time winning record on "Monday Night Football" (through 1997): the Pittsburgh Steelers or the St. Louis (and Los Angeles) Rams?

54. Where did San Francisco 49ers quarterback Steve Young play in college?

55. What are the last names of "the Marks Brothers," the former Miami Dolphins wide receivers who starred in the 1980s and early '90s?

56. With what organization did running back Jerome Bettis play the first three seasons of his NFL career (1993–95) before being traded to the Pittsburgh Steelers in 1996?

57. Name the tight end who played in seven games as a Washington Redskins rookie in 1995 before making a permanent move into the starting lineup in '96.

58. What position did Hall-of-Famer Willie Lanier play: linebacker or running back?

59. What position did Hall-of-Famer Don Maynard play: cornerback or wide receiver?

60. What was the first name (spelled correctly) of the Hall of Fame Chicago Bears fullback whose last name was Nagurski?

61. If an official folds his arms in front of his chest, what is he signaling?

62. If a kickoff clears the opposing team's goal posts, what is the ruling?

63. What AFC Central team did the New England Patriots defeat 28–3 at home in the 1996 divisional playoffs?

64. What NFC team's colors are midnight green, silver, black, and white?

65. Who is the Tampa Bay Buccaneers' all-time leader in passing yards and touchdown passes? (Hint: He played with the team from 1987 to 1992.)

66. Who coached the New Orleans Saints from 1986 through the eighth game of the '96 season?

67. What NFC team's colors are burgundy and gold?

68. What NFC team's colors are blue, red, and white?

69. After a missed field goal, if the ball was snapped from the 23-yard line and kicked from the 30, where does the opposing team take possession?

70. What NFC team's colors are dark green, gold, and white?

71. What traditional power did the Carolina Panthers defeat 26–17 at home in the 1996 NFC divisional playoffs for their first-ever postseason victory?

72. From the AFL-NFL merger in 1970 through the '97 season, which one of the following teams has a winning record in regular-season interconference play (AFC vs. NFC): the Kansas City Chiefs or the Green Bay Packers?

73. What NFC team's colors are navy blue, orange, and white?

74. What NFC team's colors are black, red, silver, and white?

75. With his sixth touchdown pass of the 1997 season, Brett Favre broke whose Green Bay Packers career record for touchdown passes?

76. What AFC team's colors are blue, green, and silver?

77. Napoleon Kaufman isn't the only running back named Napoleon in Raiders history. Who's the other?

78. What AFC team's colors are black and gold?

79. What AFC team's colors are silver and black?

80. With what AFC East team did quarterback Scott

Mitchell spend the first three years of his NFL career before signing as a free agent with the Detroit Lions in 1994?

81. What is former quarterback Boomer Esiason's actual first name: Alexander, Benjamin, Eugene, or Norman?

82. What AFC team's colors are aqua, coral, blue, and white?

83. When was wide receiver Antonio Freeman's first season in the NFL: 1992 or 1995?

84. Name any two of the four quarterbacks who started at least one game for the New Orleans Saints in 1997.

85. What AFC team's colors are orange, navy blue, and white?

86. What AFC team's colors are royal blue, scarlet red, and white?

87. Which one of the following teams has an all-time losing record on ''Monday Night Football'' (through 1997): the New Orleans Saints or the Philadelphia Eagles?

88. What AFC team's colors are black, purple, and metallic gold?

89. Name either of the teams that were involved in the highest-scoring NFL game of 1997, a 44–42 decision in week 14. (Hint: One team was from the NFC East, the other from the AFC Central.)

90. What NFC team's colors are gold and cardinal?

91. What NFC team's colors are purple, gold, and white?

92. By what nickname is quarterback Jake Plummer known?

93. What jersey number has cornerback Deion Sanders worn throughout his NFL career?

94. Name any one of the six players whose jersey numbers have been retired by the Philadelphia Eagles.

95. What NFC Central team did the Indianapolis Colts

beat 41–38 at home in their eleventh game of the 1997 season after starting the campaign 0–10?

96. From the NFL's expansion in 1995 through the '97 season, which one of the following teams had a winning record in regular-season interconference play (AFC vs. NFC): the Carolina Panthers or the Jacksonville Jaguars?

97. What team has cornerback Kevin Smith played for since being drafted in the first round in 1992?

98. What AFC team's colors are royal blue and white?

99. Which one of the following teams has an all-time losing record on "Monday Night Football" (through 1997): the Detroit Lions or the Tennessee (and Houston) Oilers?

100. Name any two of the eight players whose jersey numbers have been retired by the San Francisco 49ers.

ANSWERS

1. Memorial Stadium in Baltimore.
2. The Miami Dolphins, for whom he started all 77 games he played in and reached the Pro Bowl three times (1992, '94, and '95).
3. The Pittsburgh Steelers.
4. Number 12.
5. Grbac, whose playing career at Michigan ended in 1992.
6. The "Ickey Shuffle."
7. Lee Roy Selmon, who made six trips to the Pro Bowl in a nine-year career that ended in 1984.
8. Seifert, under whom the 49ers went 108-35-0 in eight years, to 102-63-1 in Walsh's 10 years.

9. Oklahoma State, which he left after winning the Heisman Trophy as a junior in 1988.

10. Terry Glenn of the New England Patriots, whose 90 catches eclipsed the record of 83 (by the San Francisco 49ers' Earl Cooper) that had stood since 1980.

11. "Jumpy."

12. Mike Webster.

13. The Baltimore Colts, who had led the NFL with a 13–1 record (compared to the Jets' AFL Eastern Division-leading 11–3 mark) and blown through two playoff opponents by a combined 58–14 score, and were big favorites to defeat New York.

14. Sanders, with 1,553 yards. It was his third time leading the league in that category; he did it with 1,304 yards in 1990 and 1,883 in '94.

15. The New Orleans Saints.

16. Mile High Stadium in Denver.

17. Darrell Russell of Southern Cal.

18. Sam Wyche, under whom the Bengals were 64–68 and were AFC champions in 1988.

19. Three Rivers Stadium in Pittsburgh.

20. The Raiders, who had a 65–36–1 record in games against NFC teams, compared to the Saints' 42–56–2 mark against the AFC.

21. The Chargers, who were 14–12 on Monday nights, compared to the Falcons' 5–15.

22. Rich Brooks, under whom the Rams were 13–19 in 1995 and '96.

23. Steve Largent of the Seattle Seahawks.

24. Steve Bartkowski (number 10), William Andrews (31), Jeff Van Note (57), and Tommy Nobis (60).

25. Earl Campbell of the Houston Oilers. The numbers: 1,450 yards in 1978, 1,697 in '79, a career-high 1,934 in '80, and 1,376 in '81.

26. Number 20.

27. Otto Graham (number 14), Jim Brown (32), Ernie

Davis (45), Don Fleming (46), and Lou Groza (76).

28. Pittsburgh, where he became a starter midway through his freshman season and wound up with a school-record 8,597 passing yards and 79 touchdown passes.

29. Soldier Field in Chicago. (''Soldier's'' Field is not an acceptable answer.)

30. Number 4.

31. The New York Jets, whose lone win came in week nine at the Arizona Cardinals by a score of 31–21.

32. The New England Patriots.

33. The Dallas Cowboys, with whom he started 126 games and had 94.5 sacks.

34. Tight end, at which he made four Pro Bowls.

35. The New England Patriots, who were 8–24 under MacPherson.

36. The Seattle Seahawks.

37. Erik Kramer.

38. Number 36.

39. The Pontiac Silverdome in Pontiac, Michigan.

40. Number 13.

41. The Indianapolis Colts, who were 36–36 and reached the postseason once under Meyer.

42. The Steelers, who had a 56–43 record in games against NFC teams, compared to the Cardinals' 35–48–2 mark against the AFC.

43. Johnny Unitas (number 19), Buddy Young (22), Lenny Moore (24), Art Donovan (70), Jim Parker (77), Raymond Berry (82), and Gino Marchetti (89).

44. Paul Tagliabue.

45. Earl Campbell (number 34), Jim Norton (43), Mike Munchak (63), and Elvin Bethea (65).

46. The San Francisco 49ers, by a 49–26 score over the San Diego Chargers.

47. The Buffalo Bills, with whom he had 164 receptions

for 2,537 yards and 18 touchdowns and played in three Super Bowls.

48. The Detroit Lions, with whom he started 125 of the 126 games in which he played.

49. Tony Canadeo (number 3), Don Hutson (14), Bart Starr (15), and Ray Nitschke (66).

50. The Hubert H. Humphrey Metrodome in Minneapolis. (The Metrodome is an acceptable answer.)

51. The 1983 Los Angeles Raiders, who avenged a regular-season home loss to Washington by pummeling the slightly favored Redskins 38–9 in Super Bowl XVIII.

52. Oklahoma, where over 16 seasons (1973–88) he led the Sooners to 12 Big Eight championships or co-championships and a stellar record of 157–29–4.

53. The Steelers, who were 25–17 on Monday nights, compared to the Rams' 17–20.

54. Brigham Young, where he won the Davey O'Brien Award as the nation's best quarterback in 1983, his senior season.

55. Clayton and Duper. Mark Clayton played for the team from 1983 to 1992 and is its all-time leader in receptions (550); Mark Duper played for the team from 1982 to 1992 and is its all-time leader in receiving yards (8,869).

56. The Rams—who were in Los Angeles through the 1994 season before moving to St. Louis—with whom he rushed for 3,091 yards and 13 touchdowns, was named NFL rookie of the year in '93, and played in two Pro Bowls. Somehow, after accomplishing all of that, Bettis was dealt to the Steelers along with a third-round draft pick in exchange for a second-rounder and a fourth-rounder.

57. Jamie Asher.

58. Linebacker. Lanier, who was nicknamed "Contact" for his ferocious tackling, starred for the Kansas City

Chiefs from 1967 to 1977 and was inducted into the Hall of Fame in '86.

59. Wide receiver. Maynard—who played for the New York Giants in 1958, the New York Titans from 1960 to 1962, the New York Jets from 1963 to 1972, and the St. Louis Cardinals in '73, and was inducted into the Hall of Fame in '87—had 633 receptions for 11,834 yards and 88 touchdowns in his pro career.

60. Bronko.

61. A delay of game penalty (or an excess timeout).

62. It's a touchback. (There are no points awarded to the kicking team.)

63. The Pittsburgh Steelers.

64. The Philadelphia Eagles.

65. Vinny Testaverde, with 14,820 yards and 77 touchdowns.

66. Jim Mora, who led the team to a 93–78 record and four postseason appearances before resigning.

67. The Washington Redskins.

68. The New York Giants.

69. The 30-yard line. All field goals attempted and missed from outside the 20-yard line result in the defensive team taking possession at the spot of the kick.

70. The Green Bay Packers.

71. The Dallas Cowboys.

72. The Chiefs, who had a 47–37–2 record in games against NFC teams, compared to the Packers' 39–56–3 mark against the AFC.

73. The Chicago Bears.

74. The Atlanta Falcons.

75. Bart Starr's. The Hall-of-Famer threw for 152 scores with the Packers from 1956 to 1971.

76. The Seattle Seahawks.

77. Napoleon McCallum, who played for the Los Angeles Raiders in 1986, '90, '91, '93 and '94.

78. The Pittsburgh Steelers.
79. The Oakland Raiders.
80. The Miami Dolphins.
81. Norman.
82. The Miami Dolphins.
83. It was '95, when he served the Green Bay Packers primarily as a punt returner.
84. Heath Shuler, Danny Wuerffel, Doug Nussmeier, and Billy Joe Hobert.
85. The Denver Broncos, whose navy blue officially is called "Broncos navy blue."
86. The Buffalo Bills.
87. The Saints, who were 6–12 on Monday nights, compared to the Eagles' 14–14.
88. The Baltimore Ravens.
89. The Philadelphia Eagles and Cincinnati Bengals. The Bengals scored a touchdown to take a 42–41 lead with about one minute to play at Philadelphia, but the Eagles quickly drove downfield on the ensuing possession, and Chris Boniol kicked a 31-yard field goal at the gun for the win.
90. The San Francisco 49ers, whose gold officially is called "Forty Niners gold."
91. The Minnesota Vikings.
92. "Jake the Snake."
93. Number 21.
94. Steve Van Buren (number 15), Tom Brookshier (40), Pete Retzlaff (44), Chuck Bednarik (60), Al Wistert (70), and Jerome Brown (99).
95. The Green Bay Packers, who went into the Colts game as two-touchdown favorites and winners of five in a row.
96. The Panthers, who had an 8–4 record in games against AFC teams, compared to the Jaguars' 4–8 mark against the NFC.
97. The Dallas Cowboys.

98. The Indianapolis Colts.
99. The Lions, who were 10–11–1 on Monday nights, compared to the Oilers' 11–11.
100. John Brodie (number 12), Joe Montana (16), Joe Perry (34), Jimmy Johnson (37), Hugh McElhenny (39), Charlie Krueger (70), Leo Nomellini (73), and Dwight Clark (87).

QUICK OUTS

(75 questions, five yards each)

1. What's the team record for most extra points (one-point conversions only) in a single season: 56, 66, 76, or 86?
2. Name the team that has led the league in rushing 16 times, an impressive nine times more than the next-closest club.
3. Name the Ohio State defensive tackle selected by the Cincinnati Bengals with the number one overall pick in the 1994 draft.
4. Who's the only NFL player to be named defensive player of the year and have a top-ten musical single in the same season? (Hint: It was in 1994.)
5. Safety Tyrone Braxton played for the Denver Broncos from 1987 to 1993, returned to the team in '95, and finally made his first Pro Bowl after the '97 season. With what team did he play in '94: the Miami Dolphins or the Philadelphia Eagles?
6. What AFC West team had an NFL-best 13–3 record in 1995, only to lose at home in the divisional play-offs?
7. Before Pete Carroll signed on as coach of the New England Patriots prior to the 1997 season, with what

    team did he have his only NFL head coaching experience?

8. Through the 1997 season, Kansas City Chiefs cornerback Dale Carter had two special-teams returns for touchdowns in his six-year NFL career. During which did both occur: kickoff returns or punt returns?

9. True or false: Oakland Raiders owner Al Davis had a losing record in his three seasons (1963–65) as the team's head coach.

10. Which one of the following NFLers did not play at Southern Cal: Terry Allen, Tony Boselli, Keyshawn Johnson, or Junior Seau?

11. True or false: Defensive end Bruce Smith played in the USFL before beginning his NFL career with the Buffalo Bills.

12. With what team did wide receiver Irving Fryar play the first nine seasons of his NFL career (1984–92)?

13. Who is the Washington Redskins' career rushing leader?

14. Whom did Ray Rhodes replace in 1995 as Philadelphia Eagles head coach?

15. In what facility did the Carolina Panthers play their home games in 1998?

16. True or false: Former Pittsburgh Steelers coach Chuck Noll is the only coach in NFL history with four Super Bowl wins.

17. Who preceded Dennis Green as Minnesota Vikings coach?

18. Who is the Seattle Seahawks' career leader in passing yards and touchdown passes?

19. True or false: Since the AFL began play in 1960, no AFL or NFL team ever has gone an entire game without gaining at least one first down.

20. San Francisco coach Steve Mariucci was hired by

the 49ers in 1997 after one season as coach at what university?

21. Where did Carolina Panthers quarterback Kerry Collins play in college?

22. There have been five players in NFL (and AFL) history with the last name Wade. Name any two of them.

23. With what team did Hall of Fame linebacker Jack Ham play for his entire NFL career (1971–82)?

24. True or false: Running back Edgar Bennett never has rushed for at least 1,000 yards in an NFL season.

25. In what facility did the Tennessee Oilers play their home games in 1997?

26. What jersey number does San Diego Chargers linebacker Junior Seau wear?

27. With how many NFL teams has Vince Tobin been a head coach: one, two, or three?

28. What jersey number does San Francisco 49ers wide receiver Jerry Rice wear?

29. Who coached the Cleveland Browns from 1991 to 1995, before the team moved to Baltimore and became the Ravens?

30. About which Hall of Fame lineman was the book *Fatso* written: Roosevelt Brown, Art Donovan, or Frank Gatski?

31. Name the ''undersized'' (five-foot-eleven-inch) Appalachian State outside linebacker who was drafted in the third round by the Dallas Cowboys in 1997 and went on to be one of the best rookie defenders in the NFL.

32. Doug Kotar had a solid career as a running back from 1974 to 1981 with what team: the Chicago Bears or the New York Giants?

33. Whom did Joe Bugel replace in 1997 as coach of the Oakland Raiders?

34. True or false: Former Buffalo Bills coach Marv Levy once was coach of the Kansas City Chiefs.

35. Who was the Cleveland Browns' all-time leader in receptions and receiving yards? (Hint: He played for the team from 1978 to 1990.)

36. In what facility did the Jacksonville Jaguars play their home games in 1998?

37. By what nickname was Hall of Fame halfback/end Elroy Hirsch, who starred for the Los Angeles Rams from 1949 to 1957, known?

38. True or false: Hall of Fame linebacker Ted Hendricks never played for an NFL team other than the Oakland (or Los Angeles) Raiders.

39. Who was the only person to be associated with the NFL for each of the league's first 50 seasons?

40. By what score did the Green Bay Packers defeat the New England Patriots in Super Bowl XXXI: 24–20, 31–23, 35–21, or 41–17?

41. Name the flamboyant New York Jets player who led the NFL in sacks in 1983 and '84.

42. True or false: Former Green Bay Packers wide receiver Sterling Sharpe had more than 500 receptions in his NFL career.

43. With what NFL team did Hall of Fame quarterback Bobby Layne throw for 15,710 yards and 118 touchdowns from 1950 to 1958?

44. What jersey number did Hall of Fame running back O.J. Simpson wear throughout his AFL and NFL career?

45. With what team did placekicker Pat Leahy spend his entire 18-year NFL career (1974–91), amassing a team-record 1,470 points along the way?

46. True or false: The Buffalo Bills held a halftime lead in their 30–13 loss to the Dallas Cowboys in Super Bowl XXVIII.

47. True or false: Through the 1997 season, the Tampa

Bay Buccaneers never had appeared on "Monday Night Football."

48. Who led the Buffalo Bills in rushing in 1997: rookie first-rounder Antowain Smith or veteran Pro Bowler Thurman Thomas?

49. What is Pittsburgh Steelers star linebacker Levon Kirkland's actual first name: Laramie, Lincoln, or Lorenzo?

50. For how many NFL teams has Miami Dolphins coach Jimmy Johnson worked as an assistant coach: none, one, or two?

51. In what facility did the Oakland Raiders play their home games in 1998?

52. True or false: Legendary Green Bay Packers coach Earl "Curly" Lambeau once coached the Washington Redskins.

53. What team did defensive end Reggie White play for when he topped all NFL sackers with 18 in 1988?

54. Eddie Lee Ivery had a solid career as a running back from 1979 to 1986 with what team: the Dallas Cowboys or the Green Bay Packers?

55. True or false: San Francisco 49ers quarterback Steve Young holds an accounting degree.

56. From 1977 to 1980, Dan Reeves served on legendary Dallas Cowboys coach Tom Landry's staff in what capacity: defensive coordinator, offensive coordinator, or special-teams coach?

57. Bobby Jackson had a solid career as a defensive back from 1978 to 1985 with what team: the New York Jets or the St. Louis Cardinals?

58. True or false: Hall of Fame coach Weeb Ewbank actually had a losing overall record with the New York Jets, whom he led from 1963 to 1973.

59. True or false: In the pre-NFL days of organized football, field goals once were worth five points.

60. True or false: No NFL player ever has recorded more than one safety in a single game.
61. True or false: Green Bay Packers quarterback Brett Favre is a former first-round draft pick.
62. True or false: Arizona Cardinals defensive end Simeon Rice's 12.5 sacks in 1996 was an NFL rookie record.
63. True or false: Dallas Cowboys running back Emmitt Smith is a college graduate.
64. In what facility did the Arizona Cardinals play their home games in 1998?
65. With what team did Hall of Fame guard John Hannah play his entire NFL career (1973–85)?
66. Who holds the San Francisco 49ers record for rushing yards in a season, with 1,502?
67. In what facility did the St. Louis Rams play their home games in 1998?
68. Which of the following teams was in the NFL—not the AFL—in 1969, the last season before the leagues' merger: the Buffalo Bills, Houston Oilers, Oakland Raiders, or Pittsburgh Steelers?
69. Which of the following teams was in the AFL—not the NFL—in 1969, the last season before the leagues' merger: the Atlanta Falcons, Kansas City Chiefs, Los Angeles Rams, or San Francisco 49ers?
70. In what facility did the Washington Redskins play their home games in 1998?
71. True or false: Cincinnati Bengals quarterback Jeff Blake is a former Pro Bowler.
72. Tom Pridemore had a solid career as a defensive back from 1978 to 1985 with what team: the Atlanta Falcons or the Tampa Bay Buccaneers?
73. What was longtime coach Ted Marchibroda during his NFL playing days: a center, a guard, or a quarterback?
74. True or false: Through the 1997 season, the San Di-

ego Chargers had an all-time winning record against the Seattle Seahawks.

75. True or false: The Philadelphia Eagles have an all-time winning record against the New York Giants.

ANSWERS

1. Sixty-six, by the 1984 Miami Dolphins—and it could have been more, but Uwe von Schamann failed to convert on four of his 70 point-after attempts.

2. The Chicago Bears (1932, '34, '35, '39, '40, '41, '42, '51, '55, '56, '68, '77, '83, '84, '85, and '86.)

3. Dan Wilkinson, who started 59 games and totaled 25 sacks in four seasons with the Bengals before being traded to the Washington Redskins.

4. The Dallas Cowboys' multitalented "Neon" Deion Sanders; the hit single was "Must Be the Money."

5. The Dolphins, with whom he had two interceptions.

6. The Kansas City Chiefs, who were upset by the Indianapolis Colts 10–7.

7. The New York Jets, who fired Carroll after he went 6–10 in his only season in that position with the team, 1994. Interestingly, Carroll had no experience as a head coach prior to that Jets job; he spent seven years as a college assistant at Arkansas ('77), Iowa State ('78), Ohio State ('79), North Carolina State ('80–'82), and Pacific ('83).

8. Punt returns, both of which came in his rookie season of 1992.

9. False. Davis, who turned 33 in '63, led a team that had gone 1–13 the year before to a 10–4 campaign, then followed up with seasons of 5–7–2 and 8–5–1 for a three-year mark of 23–16–3.

10. Allen, who played at Clemson.

11. False. Smith was drafted by the USFL's Baltimore Stars in 1985, but he never played a game in that league.

12. The New England Patriots. Fryar was with the Miami Dolphins from 1993 to 1995 and has been with the Philadelphia Eagles since.

13. John Riggins, who totaled 7,472 yards in nine years (1976–79 and 1981–85) with the team.

14. Rich Kotite, under whom the Eagles were 37–29–0 from 1991 to 1994.

15. Ericsson Stadium in Charlotte, North Carolina.

16. True. The Steelers won all four of their Super Bowls—IX, X, XIII, and XIV—under Noll, who was inducted into the Hall of Fame in 1993.

17. Jerry Burns, under whom the Vikings were 55–46 and made the playoffs three times from 1986 to 1991.

18. Dave Krieg, who threw for 26,132 yards and 195 touchdowns with the team from 1980 to 1991.

19. False. The AFL Denver Broncos did it in a 45–7 loss to the Houston Oilers in 1966. (Four NFL teams have done it, but none since 1942.)

20. California. Mariucci's only experience as a head coach came in 1996 with the Golden Bears, whom he led to a 6–6 record, including a 42–38 loss to Navy in the Aloha Bowl.

21. Penn State, where he swept all of the major awards as the nation's best quarterback in 1994, his senior season.

22. The five: Billy Wade (quarterback, Los Angeles Rams 1954–60, Chicago Bears 1961–66); Bob Wade (defensive back, Pittsburgh Steelers '68, Washington Redskins '69, Denver Broncos '70); Charlie Wade (wide receiver, Chicago '74, Green Bay Packers '75, Kansas City Chiefs '77); Jim Wade (halfback/defen-

sive back, New York Bulldogs '49); and Tommy
Wade (quarterback, Pittsburgh '65).

23. The Pittsburgh Steelers, with whom Ham had 32 interceptions and was an eight-time Pro Bowler.

24. False. Bennett has done it once, in 1995 as a member
of the Green Bay Packers, when he rushed for 1,067
yards on 316 carries (3.4 average).

25. The Liberty Bowl in Memphis.

26. Number 55.

27. One: the Arizona Cardinals, who hired Tobin prior
to the 1996 season, the first head coaching job of his
career at any level.

28. Number 80.

29. Bill Belichik, under whom the Browns were 37–45
and reached the postseason once (in '94).

30. Donovan, a six-foot-three-inch, 265–pound defensive tackle who played 10 of his 12 pro seasons with
the Baltimore Colts.

31. Dexter Coakley, who started all 16 games in '97 and
had 69 tackles, an interception, and a fumble recov-
ery for a touchdown.

32. The Giants, with whom Kotar amassed career marks
of 900 rushes for 3,380 yards, 126 receptions for
1,022 yards, and 21 touchdowns.

33. Mike White, under whom the Raiders were 15–17
from 1995 to 1996.

34. True. Levy had a 31–42 record as Chiefs coach from
1978 to 1982.

35. Ozzie Newsome, with 662 receptions for 7,980
yards.

36. ALLTEL Stadium in Jacksonville.

37. "Crazylegs."

38. False. Hendricks played from 1969 to 1973 with the
Baltimore Colts, in '74 with the Green Bay Packers,
and from 1975 to 1983 with the Raiders (the last two
seasons in L.A.).

39. George Halas, who started as player-coach of the Decatur Staleys in 1920 and wound up as the longtime coach and owner of the Chicago Bears.

40. Green Bay won 35–21.

41. Defensive end Mark Gastineau, with 19 in 1983 and an NFL-record 22 (since the league began keeping the statistic in 1982) in '84.

42. True. Even though Sharpe's career, which began in 1988, was cut short by a neck injury in '94, he still managed to tally 595 receptions.

43. The Detroit Lions.

44. Number 32.

45. The New York Jets.

46. True. The Bills, on the strength of a Thurman Thomas touchdown run and two Doug Christie field goals, led 13–6.

47. False—but it sure had been a while since they last did. The Buccaneers had played three times on Monday night: a 23–0 loss at the Chicago Bears in 1980, a 23–17 defeat of the Miami Dolphins at home in '82, and a 12–9 loss in overtime at the Green Bay Packers in '83.

48. Smith, with 840 yards to Thomas's 643. It was the first time in Thomas' career (since 1988) he wasn't the team's number one rusher.

49. Lorenzo. Levon is his middle name.

50. None. Johnson was an assistant in six different college programs, but never in the pros.

51. Oakland-Alameda County Coliseum in Alameda, California. (Oakland Coliseum is an acceptable answer.)

52. True. Lambeau, whose last season in Green Bay was 1949, coached the Redskins to a 10–13–1 record in 1952 and '53.

53. The Philadelphia Eagles, with whom he had 124 sacks in eight seasons before signing as a free agent

with the Green Bay Packers prior to the '93 season.

54. The Packers, with whom Ivery amassed career marks of 667 rushes for 2,933 yards, 162 receptions for 1,612 yards, and 30 touchdowns.

55. True. Young earned the degree from Brigham Young in 1994.

56. Offensive coordinator.

57. The Jets, with whom Jackson amassed career marks of 21 interceptions for 196 yards, with three touchdowns.

58. True. The Jets were 73–78–6 under Ewbank.

59. True. In 1904 field goals were changed from five points to four, and in '09 from four to three.

60. False. It's been done by one player, former Los Angeles Rams defensive end Fred Dryer, in a 24–7 defeat of the Green Bay Packers in 1973.

61. False. The Atlanta Falcons selected Favre in the second round (number 33 overall) in 1991.

62. True. The consensus NFL defensive rookie of the year matched the 12.5 sacks recorded by San Diego Chargers rookie Leslie O'Neal in 1985.

63. True. Smith earned a degree in public recreation from the University of Florida in 1996—six years after he left the school as a junior to enter the NFL draft.

64. Sun Devil Stadium in Tempe, Arizona.

65. The New England Patriots, with whom he played in eight Pro Bowls.

66. Roger Craig, who did it in 1988, when he was named the NFL's offensive player of the year.

67. The Trans World Dome at America's Center in St. Louis. (Trans World Dome is an acceptable answer.)

68. The Steelers, who have been in the NFL since their inception as the Pittsburgh Pirates in 1933.

69. The Chiefs, who were in the AFL from 1963 until

the merger (after originating as the AFL Dallas Texans in '60).

70. Jack Kent Cooke Stadium in Raljon, Maryland.

71. True. Blake played in the Pro Bowl following the 1995 season, when he threw for 3,822 yards and 28 touchdowns in his first NFL campaign as a full-time starter.

72. The Falcons, with whom he totaled 21 interceptions.

73. A quarterback. Marchibroda played in 1953, '55, and '56 with the Pittsburgh Steelers, and in '57 with the Chicago Bears. His only season as a starter was in '56 with the Steelers, when he completed 124 of 275 passes for 1,585 yards and 12 touchdowns, with 19 interceptions.

74. True. San Diego held a 20–18 advantage but had lost three straight in the series.

75. False. Through the 1997 season, New York held a 65–59–2 advantage.

TIGHT END CURLS

(50 questions, seven yards each)

1. Of the following four universities, name the one place former NFL coach Marv Levy never coached: California, New Mexico, Rutgers, and William & Mary.
2. Who was the last player to return a punt for a touchdown in a Super Bowl?
3. How many NFL rushing titles did Walter Payton win in his Hall of Fame career: one, two, three, or four?
4. Which one of these players didn't rush for at least 1,000 yards in 1995: the Kansas City Chiefs' Marcus Allen, the Chicago Bears' Rashaan Salaam, the Atlanta Falcons' Craig Heyward, or the Arizona Cardinals' Garrison Hearst?
5. What is the record for the most points scored by one team in a regular-season NFL game: 63, 68, 72, or 74?
6. Name the Green Bay Packers star of the 1930s and '40s who led the league in receptions eight times.
7. Which one of the following NFLers did not play at the University of Miami: Michael Barrow, Cortez Kennedy, Jake Reed, or Leon Searcy?
8. Name the former Denver Broncos head coach who bridged the gap from Dan Reeves, whose last season

was 1992, to Mike Shanahan, whose first season was '95.

9. Name the former Seattle Seahawks quarterback who owns the NFL record for most pass attempts by a rookie.

10. How many yards did Emmitt Smith rush for as a rookie in 1990, when he started 15 games for the Dallas Cowboys: 637, 937, 1,237, or 1,537?

11. Name any three of the four NFL teams fullback Keith Byars has played for.

12. Name the tight end who led the AFC in receptions in 1980, '81, and '82.

13. Who coached the New York Jets from 1990 to 1993 before returning as an assistant to the very team he'd been with as an assistant before taking the Jets job?

14. Who holds the Tampa Bay Buccaneers record for passing yards in a season?

15. What's the difference between ''encroachment'' and ''offsides''?

16. Who coached the Cleveland Browns from 1978 to 1984?

17. Troy Aikman is the Dallas Cowboys' career leader in passing yards, but he doesn't yet own the team record for touchdown passes. Who does?

18. What Washington Redskins player led the NFC in 1994 with 13.5 sacks?

19. With what team did star outside linebacker Joe Fortunato play for his entire 11-year NFL career (1956–66): the Chicago Bears, Cleveland Browns, or Green Bay Packers?

20. Who is the winningest coach in Kansas City Chiefs history?

21. Name the player who led the AFC in receptions in 1990, '91, and '92.

22. What player led the NFL in rushing in 1991, '92, '93, and '95?

23. Name the Minnesota Vikings player who led the NFC in receptions in 1977 and '79.

24. With what team did linebacker Lamar Lathon play his first five NFL seasons (1990–94) before signing as a free agent with the Carolina Panthers in 1995?

25. What position did Oakland Raiders Hall-of-Famer Art Shell play?

26. What team won Super Bowl XXIII on January 22, 1989?

27. How many Super Bowls did the San Francisco 49ers win with Bill Walsh as coach?

28. What Buffalo Bills player led the NFL in 1995 with 17.5 sacks?

29. Who were the two starting wide receivers for the Green Bay Packers in Super Bowl XXXI?

30. What NFL team did current New Orleans Saints coach Mike Ditka serve as an assistant coach from 1973 to 1981?

31. In what year did the Miami Dolphins record their perfect season of 14–0 (17–0 including the playoffs)?

32. With what team did star cornerback Roger Wehrli play for his entire 14-year NFL career (1969–82): the Detroit Lions, Minnesota Vikings, or St. Louis Cardinals?

33. What jersey number does Oakland Raiders wide receiver Tim Brown wear?

34. What team has led the NFL in scoring four times in the 1990s?

35. Name the former Tampa Bay Buccaneers running back who had an NFL-record 496 rushing attempts in 1984.

36. What Pittsburgh Steelers player rushed for a team-record and AFC-best 1,690 yards in 1992?

37. Who is the New England Patriots' all-time leader in passing yards and touchdown passes?

38. With what team did star wide receiver/kick returner

Rick Upchurch play for his entire nine-year NFL career (1975–83): the Baltimore Colts, Denver Broncos, or New England Patriots?

39. What New York Jets wide receiver led the AFC in receptions in 1987 and '88?

40. How does the wide receiver/kick returner whose last name is Ismail spell his first name? (Hint: His name is pronounced "KAH-dree.")

41. What Dallas Cowboys running back led the NFC in 1988 with 1,514 rushing yards?

42. When was Dallas Cowboys wide receiver Michael Irvin's first season in the NFL: 1987, '88, '89, or '90?

43. How many yards did New York Jets running back Curtis Martin rush for in his three seasons with the New England Patriots (1995–97): 3,304, 3,567, or 3,799?

44. Name the Southern Mississippi punter who was drafted in the first round by the Oakland Raiders in 1973—the only pure punter ever to be a first-rounder—and played for the Raiders until 1986.

45. What running back ran for a Pro Bowl–record 180 yards to lead the AFC to a 41–13 victory over the NFC in February 1995: Gary Brown, Marshall Faulk, Thurman Thomas, or Chris Warren?

46. What Indianapolis Colts wide receiver led the AFC in 1993 with 85 receptions?

47. What St. Louis Cardinals wide receiver led the NFL in 1987 in receptions (91) and receiving yards (1,117)? (Hint: He spent the first six seasons of his career, 1979–84, with the Kansas City Chiefs, then was with the Cardinals organization until '90.)

48. What Dallas Cowboys cornerback led the NFL in interceptions in 1981, '82, and '85?

49. For what team did safety Felix Wright play when he led the NFL in 1989 with nine interceptions?

50. What team won Super Bowl XXII on January 31, 1988?

ANSWERS

1. Rutgers; Levy coached at New Mexico in 1958 and '59, at California from 1960 to 1963, and at William & Mary from 1964 to 1968.
2. It's never been done.
3. Surprisingly enough, the NFL's all-time leading rusher won but one rushing title, with 1,852 yards in 1977.
4. Allen, who rushed for 890 yards. Salaam totaled 1,074, Heyward 1,083, and Hearst 1,070.
5. Seventy-two, by the Washington Redskins in a 72–41 defeat of the New York Giants in 1966. The teams' 113 points combined also is an NFL record for the most points scored by two teams in one game.
6. Hall-of-Famer Don Hutson, who accomplished the feat three more times than former Denver Broncos receiver Lionel Taylor and five more times than anyone else.
7. Reed, who graduated from Grambling State with a degree in criminal justice in 1991.
8. Wade Phillips, under whom the Broncos went 16–17 in '93 and '94.
9. Rick Mirer, with 486 attempts in 1993. Second on the list is another former Seahawk, Jim Zorn, who had 439 in '76.
10. Smith had 937 yards on 241 carries (a 3.9 average), with 11 touchdowns.
11. The four: the Philadelphia Eagles (1986–92), Miami Dolphins ('93 through the first four games of '96),

New England Patriots (from Week 7 of '96 through '97), and New York Jets (since '98).

12. Kellen Winslow of the San Diego Chargers, with NFL bests of 89 in 1980 and 88 in '81, and an AFC-best 54 in the strike-shortened '82 season.

13. Bruce Coslet, under whom the Jets were 26–39 and reached the playoffs once (in 1991). Coslet filled various assistant's roles with the Bengals from 1981 to 1989 and returned as their offensive coordinator in '94.

14. Doug Williams, who threw for 3,563 yards in 1981.

15. Encroachment is called when a defensive player enters the neutral zone and makes contact with an opponent before the ball is snapped; a defensive player is offsides when any part of his body is beyond the line of scrimmage when the ball is snapped.

16. Sam Rutigliano, under whom the Browns went 47–52–0 over that span.

17. Danny White, with 155.

18. Ken Harvey, an outside linebacker.

19. The Bears, with whom the six-foot, 225-pound Fortunato played in five Pro Bowls, including four consecutively (1962–65 seasons).

20. Hank Stram, under whom the Chiefs were 129–79–10 from 1960 to 1974.

21. Haywood Jeffires of the Houston Oilers, with 74 in 1990 (tied for the lead with teammate Drew Hill), 100 in '91, and 90 in '92.

22. Emmitt Smith of the Dallas Cowboys, with 1,563 in 1991, 1,713 in '92, 1,486 in '93, and 1,773 in '95.

23. Ahmad Rashad of the Minnesota Vikings, with 51 in 1977 and 80 in '79. Rashad, of course, has gone on to even bigger fame as a reporter and studio host for NBC Sports.

24. The Houston Oilers, with whom he started 44 games and had 14 sacks.

25. Offensive tackle, from 1968 to 1982 (in '82 with the Los Angeles Raiders).
26. The San Francisco 49ers, by a 20–16 score over the Cincinnati Bengals.
27. Three: Super Bowls XVI, XIX, and XXIII.
28. Bryce Paup, a linebacker who was named the league's defensive player of the year that season.
29. Antonio Freeman and Andre Rison. Rison—whom the Packers picked up late in the 1997 season after starter Robert Brooks was injured—caught a 54-yard touchdown pass 3:32 into the game and finished with two catches for 77 yards; Freeman caught three passes for 105 yards, 81 coming on a second-quarter touchdown.
30. The Dallas Cowboys, as receivers coach (1973–74), special teams/tight ends coach (1975–76, '80), and special teams/receivers coach (1977–79, '81).
31. The Dolphins did it in 1972, winning the AFC East by seven games, then defeating (in order) the Cleveland Browns, Pittsburgh Steelers, and Washington Redskins in the postseason for the title.
32. The Cardinals, with whom the six-foot, 194-pound Wehrli intercepted 40 passes and played in seven Pro Bowls.
33. Number 81.
34. The San Francisco 49ers, in 1992 (431 points), '93 (473), '94 (505), and '95 (457).
35. James Wilder, who also rushed for a team-record 1,544 yards that season.
36. Barry Foster, who played for the team from 1990 to 1994 and totaled 3,943 rushing yards.
37. Steve Grogan, who threw for 26,886 yards and 182 touchdowns with the team from 1975 to 1990.
38. The Broncos, with whom the five-foot-ten-inch, 175–pound Upchurch caught 4,369 yards worth of passes and set nearly every team kick- and punt-

return record. Upchurch's best special-teams season came in '76, when he tied an NFL record with four punt returns for touchdowns.

39. Al Toon, with 68 in 1987 and 93 in '88.

40. Qadry.

41. Herschel Walker.

42. It was 1988, when he started 10 games and totaled 32 receptions for 654 yards and five touchdowns.

43. Martin rushed for 3,799 yards with the Patriots.

44. Ray Guy, who averaged 42.3 yards a punt in his career (but was known even better for his great hang time) and who played in seven Pro Bowls.

45. Faulk. The Indianapolis Colts rookie averaged nearly 14 yards on only 13 carries and easily surpassed the previous record of 112 yards set by O.J. Simpson in the 1973 game. The Seattle Seahawks' Warren also had a spectacular game, rushing for 127 yards on only 14 carries.

46. Reggie Langhorne, who accomplished the feat in the final season of his NFL career.

47. J.T. Smith.

48. Everson Walls, with 11 in 1981 (his rookie season), seven in '82, and nine in '85.

49. The Cleveland Browns, for whom he played from 1985 to 1990.

50. The Washington Redskins, by a 42–10 score over the Denver Broncos.

GAPING HOLES

(50 questions, 10 yards each)

1. Which one of the following current star wide receivers has never reached 100 receptions in a single NFL season (through 1997): Robert Brooks, Tim Brown, Terance Mathis, or Jimmy Smith?
2. What team finished first in the AFC West in 1988 at 9–7, a mark that was worse than those of all four of the league's wild-card playoff teams?
3. In the three seasons prior to the NFL-AFL merger—1967, '68, and '69—the NFL's Eastern and Western Conferences were split into a total of four divisions. Name any two of them.
4. Name the first commissioner of the NFL.
5. Current Washington Redskins coach Norv Turner was preceded in that position by Richie Petitbon, who preceded Hall-of-Famer Joe Gibbs. Who preceded Gibbs?
6. Who won the 1992 Heisman Trophy? (Hint: He didn't exactly flourish in the NFL.)
7. The Dallas Cowboys' 30–13 defeat of the Buffalo Bills in Super Bowl XXVIII was played in what stadium?
8. With what team did defensive end Eric Curry play the first five seasons of his NFL career (1993–97)

before signing as a free agent with the Green Bay Packers in 1998?

9. Quarterback Mark Rypien's outstanding career with the Washington Redskins spanned 1988 to 1993 and included a Super Bowl most valuable player award. Since his Redskins days, though, Rypien has bounced around, playing with three different teams (through 1997). Name any two of them.

10. Tennessee Oilers coach Jeff Fisher played four years in the NFL (1981–84) as a backup safety with what team: the Buffalo Bills, Chicago Bears, or Houston Oilers?

11. What University of Georgia running back did the New York Giants select in the first round (number 24 overall) of the 1990 draft?

12. Name the former Atlanta Falcons defensive end who, since his retirement in 1993, has written books including: *The Dark Side of the Game: My Life in the NFL*; *A Man and His Mother: An Adopted Son's Search*; *Outlaws*; *Ruffians*; *The Red Zone*; and *Titans.*

13. Which team led the AFC in total offense *and* total defense in 1997?

14. What team won Super Bowl XVII on January 30, 1983?

15. Some might say Calvin Hill's best work was fathering NBA superstar Grant Hill, but the old man had quite a pro career of his own, amassing 6,083 rushing yards, 2,861 receiving yards, and 65 touchdowns from 1969 to 1981 with the Dallas Cowboys, Washington Redskins, and Cleveland Browns. At what Ivy League school did the running back play his college ball?

16. Name any one of the three men who coached the New England Patriots during their first decade of existence, the 1960s.

17. Whom did Wayne Fontes replace as Detroit Lions coach 12 games into the 1988 season?

18. In what year did the Houston (now Tennessee) Oilers make Alcorn State quarterback Steve McNair their first-round draft pick (number three overall)?

19. What two head coaching jobs has current Miami Dolphins coach Jimmy Johnson had at the college level?

20. Who holds the Buffalo Bills record for most passing yards in a single game? (Hint: It isn't Jim Kelly.)

21. How many seasons did it take Mike Holmgren as Green Bay Packers coach to win the NFC Central title?

22. Where did fullback Mike Alstott play in college: Boston College, Notre Dame, or Purdue?

23. Spell either the first or the last name of San Francisco 49ers wide receiver/punt returner Iheanyi Uwaezuoke (pronounced "E-HAHN-E ooh-WAY-zoo-kay"), who was born in Nigeria and moved to Inglewood, California, at the age of seven.

24. Who is the leading passer in Atlanta Falcons history?

25. What jersey number does Tennessee Oilers running back Eddie George wear?

26. What team had an NFL-best 15–1 record in 1985?

27. What team did the Dallas Cowboys defeat in Super Bowl XII?

28. Which *two* of the following teams have an all-time winning record on NFL opening day: the Buffalo Bills, Chicago Bears, Denver Broncos, and Philadelphia Eagles?

29. Who is the only Miami Dolphins player ever to have his jersey retired by the team?

30. San Francisco 49ers wide receiver Jerry Rice holds the NFL record for most consecutive regular-season games with at least one touchdown reception, with how many: 9, 11, 13, or 15?

31. Hall of Fame running back Tony Dorsett, who played for the Dallas Cowboys from 1977 to 1987, finished his NFL career in '88 with what team?

32. Which coach holds the all-time NFL record for post-season victories, with 20: Tom Landry, Chuck Noll, or Don Shula?

33. What NFL team did Vince Lombardi coach for one season, 1969, his final in the league?

34. With what NFL team did wide receiver Keenan McCardell play for four seasons (1992–95) before signing as a free agent with the Jacksonville Jaguars in 1996?

35. How many times has Denver Broncos quarterback John Elway thrown for at least 4,000 yards in an NFL season: none, once, three times, or five times?

36. Name the future NFL star quarterback who finished second to running back Herschel Walker in the 1982 Heisman Trophy balloting.

37. What jersey number does New England Patriots tight end Ben Coates wear?

38. Linebacker Jeff Brady, a twelfth-round draft pick out of Kentucky in 1991, traveled a journeyman's road before finally finding a home with the Minnesota Vikings in 1995. Name any one of the five NFL teams with which Brady played before signing with Minnesota.

39. What jersey number does Denver Broncos tight end Shannon Sharpe wear?

40. Over eight seasons from 1990 to 1997, how many different players led the New Orleans Saints in rushing for at least one season: five, six, or seven?

41. Which "D" holds the NFL record for most rushing yards gained in a playoff game: Terrell Davis, Eric Dickerson, or Tony Dorsett?

42. Who coached the Houston Oilers from 1985 to 1989?

43. Who is the oldest quarterback ever to lead his team to a Super Bowl: John Elway, Bart Starr, or Johnny Unitas?

44. What team won Super Bowl XVI on January 24, 1982?

45. What is wide receiver Andre Rison's middle name: Brevin, Previn, or Trevin?

46. Name any one of the six men who coached the Houston Oilers during their first decade of existence, the 1960s.

47. Who is the only head coach in NFL history to lose a Super Bowl with two different teams?

48. Name the current AFC kicker who holds the record for the longest field goal in Super Bowl history.

49. Wide receiver Keyshawn Johnson asked to wear jersey number 3 (his college number) when the New York Jets made him the number one overall pick in the 1996 draft, but his request was denied because the NFL reserves such low jersey numbers for quarterbacks, kickers, and punters. What number did he wind up wearing?

50. Name the former quarterback who is the only player in NFL history to be named most valuable player of the Super Bowl three times.

ANSWERS

1. Smith. His high—83—came in 1996, his second season with the Jacksonville Jaguars. The other three have reached 100 once apiece: Brooks (102) in '95 with the Green Bay Packers, Brown (104) in '97 with the Oakland Raiders, and Mathis (111) in '94 with the Atlanta Falcons.

2. The Seattle Seahawks, who went on to lose 21–13 to the Cincinnati Bengals in the divisional playoffs.

3. The Eastern Conference was split into the Capital and Century Divisions; the Western Conference was split into the Coastal and Central Divisions.

4. Elmer Layden, who was named to the post on March 1, 1941.

5. Jack Pardee, who held that position from 1978 to 1980.

6. University of Miami quarterback Gino Torretta, who through 1997 had filled nonstarter's roles for brief stints with the Minnesota Vikings, Seattle Seahawks, and Detroit Lions.

7. Atlanta's Georgia Dome.

8. The Tampa Bay Buccaneers, with whom the former first-round draft pick (number six overall) started 44 games and registered 12 sacks.

9. The three: the Cleveland Browns, with whom he had three starts and seven games played in 1994; the St. Louis Rams, with whom he had three starts and 16 games played in '95 and '97; and the Philadelphia Eagles, with whom he had no starts and one game played in '96.

10. The Bears, for whom Fisher also was the number one punt returner in '81 and '84.

11. Rodney Hampton, who was a Pro Bowler by the 1992 season.

12. Tim Green, a 1986 first-round draft choice by Atlanta who totaled 24 sacks in 99 games in his career.

13. The eventual Super Bowl champion Denver Broncos, who were the first team to accomplish that since the 1979 Pittsburgh Steelers.

14. The Washington Redskins, by a 27–17 score over the Miami Dolphins.

15. Yale, where he played so well that the Cowboys

made him their first-round draft pick in 1969.

16. Lou Saban (1960–61), Mike Holovak (1961–68), and Clive Rush (1969).

17. Darryl Rogers, under whom the Lions were 18–40 from 1985 through the first 11 games of '88.

18. McNair was drafted in 1995.

19. Johnson coached Oklahoma State from 1979 to 1983 and the University of Miami from 1984 to 1988. His overall college record was 81–34–3 and included a national championship at Miami in '87.

20. Joe Ferguson, who threw for 419 yards in a 38–35 overtime defeat of the Miami Dolphins in 1983.

21. Four. The Packers finished either second or tied for second at 9–7 in each of Holmgren's first three seasons in Green Bay (1992, '93, and '94); they won the Central at 11–5 in '95.

22. Purdue, where the 1996 Tampa Bay Buccaneers draftee rushed for 3,635 yards in his career and was named the Boilermakers' most valuable player each of his last three seasons (1993–95).

23. Iheanyi Uwaezuoke.

24. Steve Bartkowski, who threw for 23,468 yards in 11 seasons (1975–85) with the team.

25. Number 27.

26. The Chicago Bears, who went on to blow out the New England Patriots 46–10 in Super Bowl XX.

27. The Denver Broncos, by a 27–10 score.

28. Chicago and Denver. Through the 1997 season, the Broncos were 24–13–1, the Bears 38–26–1, the Bills 16–22–0, and the Eagles 26–36–1.

29. Bob Griese, number 12, who played quarterback for the team from 1967 to 1980, throwing for 25,092 yards and 192 touchdowns.

30. Thirteen, from the last game of the 1986 season to the last game of the '87 season. (Rice played in only 12 games in '87.)

31. The Denver Broncos, for whom he rushed for 703 yards on 181 carries (3.9 average) and scored five touchdowns.

32. Landry, whose Dallas Cowboys compiled 20 wins during his tenure as coach. Shula finished his career with 19 playoff wins; Noll finished with 16.

33. The Washington Redskins, who were 7–5–2 that season, the first time since 1955 they'd been better than .500.

34. The Cleveland Browns, with whom McCardell had 80 receptions for eight touchdowns.

35. Once: in 1993, when he threw for an NFL-high 4,030 yards.

36. John Elway.

37. Number 87.

38. The teams: the Pittsburgh Steelers in 1991, Green Bay Packers in '92, Los Angeles Rams and San Diego Chargers in '93, and Tampa Bay Buccaneers in '94.

39. Number 84.

40. Six: Craig Heyward in 1990 (with 599 yards), Fred McAfee in '91 (494), Vaughn Dunbar in '92 (565), Derek Brown in '93 (705), Mario Bates in '94 (579), Bates in '95 (951), Bates in '96 (584), and Ray Zellars in '97 (552).

41. Dickerson, who gained 248 yards for the Los Angeles Rams in a 20–0 home victory over the Dallas Cowboys in the 1985 NFC divisional playoffs.

42. Jerry Glanville, under whom the Oilers were 35–35 and reached the playoffs three times.

43. Unitas, who was 37 years, eight months when the Baltimore Colts beat the Dallas Cowboys 16–13 in Super Bowl V—about a month older than Elway was when he led the Denver Broncos to victory in Super Bowl XXXII. Starr had just turned 34 when the Green Bay Packers won Super Bowl II.

44. The San Francisco 49ers, by a 26–21 score over the Cincinnati Bengals.
45. Previn.
46. Lou Rymkus (1960–61), Wally Lemm ('61), Frank "Pop" Ivy ('62–63), Sammy Baugh ('64), Hugh Taylor ('65), and Wally Lemm ('66–69).
47. Don Shula, with the Baltimore Colts in Super Bowl III and the Miami Dolphins in Super Bowls VI, XVII, and XIX.
48. Steve Christie of Buffalo, who kicked a 54-yarder for the Bills in Super Bowl XXVII.
49. Number 19. High-teens numbers are allowed for receivers only when a team has no available numbers in the 80s, which was the case—after a little creative maneuvering—with the Jets.
50. Joe Montana of the San Francisco 49ers, who was named MVP of Super Bowls XVI, XIX, and XXIV.

CROSSING ROUTES

(50 questions, 15 yards each)

1. For how many seasons did quarterback Warren Moon play with the Edmonton Eskimos of the Canadian Football League: four, five, six, or seven?
2. Of the following players, name the one who wasn't in the NFL in 1985: tight end Pete Metzelaars, quarterback Mike Tomczak, cornerback Albert Lewis, and running back Ronnie Harmon.
3. After how many seasons with the Green Bay Packers—a team he joined prior to the 1992 season—did quarterback Brett Favre make his first trip to the Pro Bowl?
4. Who holds the Washington Redskins' single-season record for passing yards, with 4,109?
5. Which running back had the most regular-season receptions in the five-year period ending in 1997: Kimble Anders, Emmitt Smith, or Ricky Watters?
6. In whose honor have the Seattle Seahawks retired jersey number 12?
7. Whom did Marty Schottenheimer replace in 1989 as Kansas City Chiefs head coach?
8. What team won the NFC East in 1989 with a 12–4 record?
9. What team did the Washington Redskins defeat in

the NFC Championship Game the last time they won
the Super Bowl?

10. Minnesota Vikings coach Dennis Green served as an
assistant for what NFL team in 1979 and again from
1986 to 1988?

11. Where did quarterback Neil O'Donnell play in college: Colorado, Maryland, or West Virginia?

12. What current NFL team originated as the Dallas Texans?

13. How tall (within one inch either way) was the tallest
player in NFL history?

14. What quarterback led the NFL in 1994 in completions (400), attempts (691), passing yards (4,555),
and interceptions thrown (27)?

15. Hall of Fame cornerback Mike Haynes is best-known
for his accomplishments as a Los Angeles Raider
from 1983 to 1989, but with what NFL team did he
play—and play extremely well—from 1976 to 1982?

16. Name the head coach who lasted all of one season
(1990) with the New England Patriots.

17. The 1962 Houston Oilers hold the single-season record (NFL or AFL) for passes intercepted by their
opponents, with how many: 34, 38, 44, or 48?

18. According to the NFL rule book, how many approved footballs must be on hand for games played
outdoors: 12, 24, 36, or 48?

19. Who is the NFL's all-time leader in interceptions,
with 81?

20. What team did the Green Bay Packers defeat 23–20
in overtime on ''Monday Night Football'' in 1996
on a 53-yard field goal by Chris Jacke—incidentally,
Jacke's only field-goal attempt of 50 or more yards
all season?

21. Starting with what season did the NFL make the
switch from a 14–game schedule to a 16–game
schedule: 1972, '74, '76, or '78?

22. Who was the oldest coach in the NFL in 1997?

23. What team from 1971 to 1974 set the NFL record for consecutive home wins, with 27?

24. In 1965, the AFL won a bidding war over the NFL when the New York Jets signed University of Alabama quarterback Joe Namath to the largest rookie contract in pro football history. What was the deal worth: $127,000; $427,000; or $727,000?

25. In 1991 the top five rushers in the AFC played for the Buffalo Bills, Denver Broncos, Kansas City Chiefs, New England Patriots, and Miami Dolphins. Name any three of them.

26. Of the following teams—the Baltimore Colts, Cleveland Browns, and San Francisco 49ers—how many were part of the All-America Football Conference, which was alive from 1946 to 1949?

27. Name the San Diego Chargers running back who led the AFC in rushing in 1984 with 1,179 yards. (Hint: He later played for the Philadelphia Eagles and Pittsburgh Steelers.)

28. What team did the Buffalo Bills defeat 30–13 in the 1993 AFC Championship Game (played January 23, 1994)?

29. Who was coach of the Cincinnati Bengals in 1981, when they won the AFC Central with a 12–4 record and advanced to the Super Bowl?

30. How many NFL teams had a better regular-season record in 1978 than the Pittsburgh Steelers, who went on to win the Super Bowl?

31. How many jersey numbers have the Dallas Cowboys retired: none, one, three, or six?

32. Where did Hall of Fame quarterback Roger Staubach play in college?

33. What team won Super Bowl X on January 18, 1976?

34. The Pro Football Hall of Fame Class of 1995 consists of five men: one affiliated with the Tampa Bay

Buccaneers; one with the Seattle Seahawks; one with the San Diego Chargers; one with the Cleveland Browns and Green Bay Packers; and one with the Minnesota Vikings, Chicago Bears, and New Orleans Saints. Name any of the five.

35. What is the nickname of 10-year NFL veteran wide receiver Willie Lee Anderson Jr., who spent the 1997 season with the Denver Broncos?

36. In 1983 the top five rushers in the NFC played for the Los Angeles Rams, Atlanta Falcons, Chicago Bears, Washington Redskins, and Dallas Cowboys. Name any four of them.

37. There have been three players in NFL history with the last name Agee. Name any one of them.

38. Who is the Kansas City Chiefs' all-time leader in receptions?

39. What was the Los Angeles Rams' all-time record in the Super Bowl?

40. The San Francisco 49ers had a pair of brothers named Fahnhorst—one a tackle, the other a linebacker—who between them played for the team from 1974 to 1990 (their careers overlapped from 1984 to 1987). Name either one of them.

41. In how many of Hall of Fame quarterback Sammy Baugh's 16 NFL seasons did he throw for at least 1,000 yards? (An answer within one season either way of the actual number counts as correct.)

42. Punter Mike Bragg didn't miss a single start in his 13-year NFL career, the first 12 years of which—a total of 172 regular-season games—were spent with the same team. What team did he punt for from 1968 to 1979: the Chicago Bears, Detroit Lions, or Washington Redskins?

43. Who coached the Minnesota Vikings from their inception in 1961 to '66?

44. The 1966 Los Angeles Rams and 1971 Washington

Redskins co-hold the all-time NFL record for most field goals attempted in a season, with how many: 44, 49, 54, or 59?

45. What is the NFL team record for most first downs rushing in a single game: 20, 25, 30, or 35?

46. Name both teams quarterback Bobby Hebert played for during his 11-year NFL career (1985–89, 1991–96).

47. What was the name of the facility in which the Washington Redskins played their home games from 1937 to 1960: Abner Field, Capitol Park, or Griffith Stadium?

48. What is the NFL team record for most first downs passing in a single game: 19, 24, 29, or 34?

49. In what facility did the New York Giants play their home games from 1925 to 1955?

50. Where did San Francisco 49ers wide receiver Jerry Rice play in college?

ANSWERS

1. Six (1978 through '83), over which he threw for a whopping 21,228 yards and 144 touchdowns.

2. Harmon, who was the Buffalo Bills' first-round draft pick in 1986. Metzelaars entered the league in 1982, Tomczak in '85, and Lewis in '83.

3. One. Favre, who never even completed a pass in his 1991 rookie season with the Atlanta Falcons, started 13 games (and played in 15) with the Packers in '92 and completed 302 of 471 passes for 3,227 yards and 18 touchdowns.

4. Jay Schroeder, who accomplished the feat in 1986,

his only full season as the team's starting quarter-back.

5. Anders, with 281 (all with the Kansas City Chiefs), including a career-high 67 in 1994. Watters had 258 (with the San Francisco 49ers and Philadelphia Eagles), including a career-high 66 in '94; Smith had 256 (all with the Dallas Cowboys), including a career-high 62 in '95.

6. Their fans, the "12th man."

7. Frank Gansz, who compiled an 8–22–1 record during his two seasons (1987 and '88) with the Chiefs.

8. The New York Giants, who were upset 19–13 in overtime by the wild-card Los Angeles Rams in the divisional playoffs.

9. The Detroit Lions, by a 41–10 score at RFK Stadium January 12, 1992. The Redskins went on to hammer the Buffalo Bills 37–24 in Super Bowl XXVI.

10. The San Francisco 49ers, as special-teams coach in '79 and as receivers coach from 1986 to 1988.

11. Maryland, where he threw for 4,989 yards and 26 touchdowns in his two years (1988 and '89) as a starter.

12. The Kansas City Chiefs. The Texans—who were one of the original AFL teams in 1960—moved to Kansas City, Missouri, and became the Chiefs in February 1963.

13. A seven-foot, 300-pound defensive tackle named Richard Sligh played in eight games with the Oakland Raiders as a rookie in 1967 after being drafted in the tenth round out of North Carolina Central.

14. Drew Bledsoe of the New England Patriots, who also threw 25 touchdown passes.

15. The New England Patriots, with whom he won AFC rookie of the year honors, played in six Pro Bowls, and recorded 28 of his 46 career interceptions.

16. Rod Rust, who went 1–15 before being fired.

17. Forty-eight. Somehow, the Oilers still managed to win the AFL Eastern Division title with an 11–3 record.

18. Thirty-six. There must be at least 24 approved balls for indoor games.

19. Paul Krause, who had 28 INTs in four seasons (1964–67) with the Washington Redskins and 53 INTs in 12 seasons (1968–79) with the Minnesota Vikings.

20. The San Francisco 49ers.

21. The first season was 1978.

22. Marv Levy of the Buffalo Bills, who was 72 and in his final NFL season. Levy was born August 3, 1925, in Chicago.

23. The Miami Dolphins, whose streak finally ended when they lost 31–21 to the Oakland Raiders in the 1975 home opener.

24. It was worth $427,000.

25. The five, in order: Thurman Thomas (1,407 yards), Gaston Green (1,037), Christian Okoye (1,031), Leonard Russell (959), and Mark Higgs (905).

26. All three—and all three were absorbed by the NFL in time for the 1950 season.

27. Earnest Jackson, who rushed for 4,167 yards in his career with the Chargers (1983 and '84), Eagles (1985), and Steelers (1986–88).

28. The Kansas City Chiefs. Buffalo led only 7–6 after one quarter and 20–13 after three, but then put the game away with a Doug Christie field goal and a Thurman Thomas touchdown run.

29. Forrest Gregg, who coached the team for four years (1980–83) and went 34–27.

30. None. The Steelers capped a 14–2 season by defeating the Dallas Cowboys 35–31 in Super Bowl XIII.

31. Surprisingly, none.

32. Navy.

33. The Pittsburgh Steelers, by a 21–17 score over the Dallas Cowboys.

34. The five, in order: defensive end Lee Roy Selmon, wide receiver Steve Largent, tight end Kellen Winslow, defensive tackle Henry Jordan, and administrator Jim Finks.

35. "Flipper."

36. The five, in order: Eric Dickerson (1,808 yards), William Andrews (1,567), Walter Payton (1,421), John Riggins (1,347), and Tony Dorsett (1,321).

37. The three: Sam, a fullback who played for the Chicago Cardinals from 1938 to 1939; Tommie, a running back who played for the Seattle Seahawks ('88), Kansas City Chiefs ('89), and Dallas Cowboys (1990–94); and Mel, a defensive lineman who played for the Indianapolis Colts (1991–92) and Atlanta Falcons (1993–95).

38. Henry Marshall, who caught 416 passes with the team from 1976 to 1987.

39. The Rams were 0–1, falling 31–19 to the Pittsburgh Steelers in Super Bowl XIV.

40. Keith, the tackle, played from 1974 to 1987; Jim, the linebacker, played from 1984 to 1990.

41. Twelve, with an average in those 1,000-yard-plus seasons of 1,626.

42. The Redskins, with whom he punted 898 times for 35,746 yards, a 39.8-yard average.

43. Norm Van Brocklin, under whom the Vikings were 29–51–4.

44. Forty-nine.

45. Twenty-five, by the Philadelphia Eagles in a 35–21 win at the Washington Redskins in 1951.

46. The New Orleans Saints (1985–1989 and 1991–1992), with whom he threw for 14,630 yards and 85 touchdowns, and the Atlanta Falcons ('93–96), with whom he threw for 7,053 yards and 50 TDs.

47. Griffith Stadium.
48. Twenty-nine, by the New York Giants in a 35–30 loss at the Cincinnati Bengals in 1985.
49. The Polo Grounds.
50. Mississippi Valley State, where he had 1,845 receiving yards and 28 touchdowns as a senior in 1984 and set 18 NCAA Division II records during his four-year career.

POST PATTERNS

(50 questions, 20 yards each)

1. The Pro Football Hall of Fame Class of 1993 consists of five men: one affiliated with the Pittsburgh Steelers; one with the San Francisco 49ers; one with the Chicago Bears; one with the San Diego Chargers; and one with the Chargers and Miami Dolphins. Name any of the five.

2. The Washington Redskins' Darrell Green and the Minnesota Vikings' John Randle are products of the same college football program. Name the school both All-Pro defenders attended. (Hint: It's in Texas.)

3. Name the San Diego Chargers quarterback who led the NFL in passing yards (3,075) and touchdown tosses (21) in 1971.

4. What's the first name, spelled correctly, of the Arizona Cardinals' three-time Pro Bowl cornerback (through 1997) whose last name is Williams?

5. Which one of the following former New Orleans Saints quarterbacks wasn't a most valuable player of the Sugar Bowl in college: Archie Manning, Bobby Scott, Ken Stabler, or Richard Todd?

6. How many games did quarterback Stan Humphries start during his four years with the Washington Redskins (1988–91): none, five, nine, or 13?

7. In the Oakland Raiders' Super Bowl season of 1980, they finished second in the AFC West behind what team?

8. What NFL season was it for Los Angeles Rams defensive back Dick "Night Train" Lane when he set the still-standing league record for interceptions in a season, with 14: his first, third, fifth, or seventh?

9. What NFL player used to be known as Sharman Shah: Karim Abdul-Jabbar, Tshimanga Biakabutuka, Hicham El-Mashtoub, or Raghib "Rocket" Ismail?

10. Name the AFC quarterback who, during a 26–20 overtime defeat of the Minnesota Vikings at home in 1994, set the all-time NFL single-game record with 70 pass attempts.

11. Name the player who was a five-time Super Bowl champion with the San Francisco 49ers (in 1988 and '89) and Dallas Cowboys (1992, '93, and '95).

12. Who was the only kicker selected in the 1997 NFL draft? (Hint: He played in the Big Ten.)

13. Name all four NFL teams, in order, for which wide receiver Desmond Howard has played since winning the Heisman Trophy in 1991.

14. Which team had the highest home attendance total in 1996: the Arizona Cardinals, Cincinnati Bengals, Oakland Raiders, or Tampa Bay Buccaneers?

15. When the Dallas Cowboys went 7–9 in 1986, it ended their NFL-record string of consecutive winning seasons at how many: 14, 17, 20, or 23?

16. Larry Allen was a Division II star in California in 1993, a starting guard with the Dallas Cowboys by midway through the '94 season, and a two-time Pro Bowler by the '96 campaign. Where did he play his college ball: California-Davis, Chico State, or Sonoma State?

17. How many seasons did Tom Landry spend as Dallas Cowboys head coach: 19, 24, 29, or 34?

18. Hall-of-Famer Norm Van Brocklin holds the NFL single-game record for most yards passing with how many: 554, 594, 654, or 694?

19. When an official extends one open hand forward, what penalty is he signaling?

20. Who coached the Seattle Seahawks from their inception in 1976 through the second game of the '82 season, after which he was fired?

21. Who had the longest tenure as head coach in New York Giants history?

22. What's the NFL record for touchdown passes by one player in a single game?

23. What team won Super Bowl IX on January 12, 1975?

24. Of the following special-teams standouts of the 1990s, who is the only one to lead the NFL in kickoff-return average and punt-return average in the same season: Mel Gray, Desmond Howard, Tyrone Hughes, or Eric Metcalf?

25. Name the star quarterback who played for the San Francisco 49ers in 1956, the Pittsburgh Steelers from 1957 to 1958, the Detroit Lions from 1958 to 1964, the New York Giants from 1965 to 1967, the Baltimore Colts from 1968 to 1971, and the Miami Dolphins from 1972 to 1976.

26. The 1978 San Francisco 49ers hold the NFL record for most turnovers committed in one season, with how many: 53, 58, 63, or 68?

27. How many losing seasons did Mike Ditka have in his 11 seasons (1982–92) as Chicago Bears coach?

28. Of the 122 games quarterback Randall Cunningham played in during his 11 seasons (1985–95) with the Philadelphia Eagles, how many did he start: 87, 97, 107, or 117?

29. Name the NFC West player who led that conference in rushing in 1985 with 1,719 yards.

30. Name the running back who played from 1981 to 1983 with the San Diego Chargers, from 1984 to 1991 with the Cincinnati Bengals, in '92 with the Cleveland Browns, and later in '92 with the Tampa Bay Buccaneers. (Hint: He's the Bengals' career rushing leader, with 6,447 yards.)

31. Who holds the Cincinnati Bengals record for touchdowns in a season, with 17?

32. How does the Pittsburgh Steelers' perennial All-Pro center whose last name is Dawson spell his first name?

33. Name any three of the six last-place teams in the NFL in 1986.

34. When was the last time the New Orleans Saints were in the playoffs?

35. For how many seasons did the Raiders play in Los Angeles: 11, 12, 13, or 14?

36. What NFL team has retired the most jersey numbers?

37. Which one of the following Pro Football Hall-of-Famers was not an offensive lineman: Forrest Gregg, Jim Langer, Larry Little, or Ernie Stautner?

38. What is Hall of Fame quarterback Bart Starr's full name?

39. Name the Kansas City Chiefs wide receiver who led the AFC in receiving yards in 1983 and '87.

40. For how many seasons did cornerback Deion Sanders play with his first NFL team, the Atlanta Falcons?

41. Which longtime AFC quarterback was selected by the Kansas City Royals in the fourth round of the 1979 free-agent baseball draft?

42. Kicker Brad Daluiso played for three NFL teams before signing with the New York Giants in 1993. Name any one of them.

43. In what country was seven-time Pro Bowl kicker Morten Andersen of the Atlanta Falcons born?

44. What is Denver Broncos quarterback John Elway's middle name: Albert, Eugene, Morris, or Nathan?

45. Hall of Fame running back John Riggins is best known for his exploits as a member of the Washington Redskins, but what was his first NFL team?

46. What jersey number does Washington Redskins cornerback Darrell Green wear?

47. Name any one of the three last-place teams in the AFC in 1988.

48. What player holds the record for receiving yards in a Super Bowl game: Cliff Branch, Jerry Rice, or Ricky Sanders?

49. Name the star quarterback who played with the Dallas Cowboys from 1965 to 1974, the New York Giants from 1974 to 1976, and the Denver Broncos from 1977 to 1982?

50. There are three Baldinger brothers—all linemen—who played in the NFL in the 1980s and '90s. Name any one of them.

ANSWERS

1. The five, in order: coach Chuck Noll, coach Bill Walsh, running back Walter Payton, quarterback Dan Fouts, and guard Larry Little.

2. Texas A&I.

3. John Hadl, who would be replaced two seasons later by a 22-year-old rookie named Dan Fouts.

4. Aeneas.

5. Manning, who played for the Saints from 1971 to 1982 and at Mississippi in college. Scott played for the Saints from 1973 to 1981 after winning a Sugar Bowl with Tennessee; Stabler (Saints 1982–84) and

Todd (1984–85) won Sugar Bowls with Alabama.

6. Five, all in 1990 when regular starter Mark Rypien was out with a knee injury. Humphries appeared in two other games that season, but he had no starts and only two appearances (both in '88) the other three years combined.

7. The San Diego Chargers. Both teams finished 11–5, but the Chargers won the division on a tie-breaker. The wild-card Raiders got their revenge by defeating the Chargers 34–27 in the AFC Championship Game.

8. His first, 1952. Lane played only one more year with the Rams, then played six seasons each with the Chicago Cardinals and Detroit Lions. He finished his NFL career with 68 interceptions, posting his second-highest total (10) in '54.

9. Abdul-Jabbar, who changed his name while in college at UCLA.

10. Drew Bledsoe of the New England Patriots, who completed 45 of those 70 passes for 426 yards and three touchdowns—and, believe it or not, no interceptions.

11. Charles Haley, a defensive end.

12. Penn State's Brett Conway, by the Green Bay Packers in the third round. Conway, the team's intended starter, didn't even last the preseason before being replaced by undrafted rookie Ryan Longwell.

13. The Washington Redskins (1992–94), the Jacksonville Jaguars ('95), the Green Bay Packers ('96), and the Oakland Raiders (since '97).

14. Oakland, with 398,915, an average of 49,864 a game (22nd in the NFL). Cincinnati ranked 24th with 382,324 (47,791 a game), Tampa Bay ranked 27th with 333,350 (41,669), and Arizona ranked 28th with 320,508 (40,064).

15. Twenty. It still stands as the third-longest such streak

in American pro sports history; the New York Yankees had a 39-year run of winning seasons from 1926 to 1964, and the Montreal Canadiens had a 32-year run from 1952 to 1983.

16. Sonoma State in Rohnert Park, California.

17. Twenty-nine. Landry coached the Cowboys from 1960, their first season, to '88, compiling a 270–178–6 record and winning two Super Bowls.

18. Van Brocklin threw for 554 yards for the Los Angeles Rams in a 54–14 defeat of the New York Yanks in 1951.

19. Illegal contact by a defensive player on a pass receiver.

20. Jack Patera, under whom the Seahawks were 35–59.

21. Steve Owen, who co-coached the team (with Benny Friedman) for the last two games of the 1930 season, then held the job on his own through 1953, compiling a 155–108–17 career record.

22. Seven. It's been done once each by five quarterbacks: the Chicago Bears' Sid Luckman in 1943, the Philadelphia Eagles' Adrian Burk in '54, the Houston Oilers' George Blanda in '61, the New York Giants' Y.A. Tittle in '62, and the Minnesota Vikings' Joe Kapp in '69.

23. The Pittsburgh Steelers, by a 16–6 score over the Minnesota Vikings.

24. Gray, who did it as a member of the Detroit Lions in 1991 with averages of 25.8 yards on kickoff returns and a career-high 15.4 yards on punt returns.

25. Earl Morral, who threw for 20,809 yards, 161 touchdowns, and 148 interceptions in his 21-year NFL career.

26. The 49ers had 63 turnovers in 16 games, an average of 3.94 a game. Not surprisingly, the team went 2–14 that season.

27. Three. The Bears were 106–62 in the regular season

under Ditka, but they were 3–6 in the strike-shortened 1982 season, 6–10 in '89, and 5–11 in '92.

28. Cunningham started 107 games for the Eagles, including all 94 he played in from 1987 to 1994.

29. Gerald Riggs of the Atlanta Falcons.

30. James Brooks, who rushed for 7,962 yards and had 3,621 yards receiving in his career.

31. Wide receiver Carl Pickens, who set the mark in 1995.

32. Dermontti.

33. The 3–13 Indianapolis Colts (AFC East), 5–11 Houston Oilers (AFC Central), 4–12 San Diego Chargers (AFC West), 4–11–1 St. Louis Cardinals (NFC East), 2–14 Tampa Bay Buccaneers (NFC Central), and 7–9 New Orleans Saints (NFC West).

34. The 1992 Saints were 12–4 and made the playoffs as a wild card.

35. Thirteen (1982–94).

36. The Chicago Bears, with 13: numbers 3 (Bronko Nagurski), 5 (George McAfee), 7 (George Halas), 28 (Willie Galimore), 34 (Walter Payton), 40 (Gale Sayers), 41 (Brian Piccolo), 42 (Sid Luckman), 51 (Dick Butkus), 56 (Bill Hewitt), 61 (Bill George), 66 (Bulldog Turner), and 77 (Red Grange).

37. Stautner, who played defensive tackle for the Pittsburgh Steelers from 1950 to 1963.

38. Bryan Bartlett Starr.

39. Carlos Carson, with 1,351 in 1983 and 1,044 in '87.

40. Five—1989–93—before he was signed as a free agent by the San Francisco 49ers.

41. Dan Marino of the Miami Dolphins, who never signed with the Royals.

42. Daluiso played for the Atlanta Falcons for the first two games of 1991, for the Buffalo Bills for the final 14 games of that season, and for the Denver Broncos in '92.

43. Denmark.
44. Albert.
45. The New York Jets, for whom Riggins played from his rookie season of 1971 to '75, rushing for 3,880 yards and 25 touchdowns along the way.
46. Number 28.
47. The 6–10 Miami Dolphins (AFC East), 5–11 Pittsburgh Steelers (AFC Central), and 4–11–1 Kansas City Chiefs (AFC West).
48. Rice, with 215 yards (on 11 receptions) in the San Francisco 49ers' win in Super Bowl XXIII.
49. Craig Morton, who threw for 27,908 yards, 183 touchdowns, and 187 interceptions in his 18-year NFL career.
50. The Baldingers (of Massapequa, New York): Brian, a center/guard/tackle who played for the Dallas Cowboys (1982–87), Indianapolis Colts (1988–91), and Philadelphia Eagles (1992–93); Gary, a defensive end/nose tackle who played for the Kansas City Chiefs (1986–88), Indianapolis Colts (1990), and Buffalo Bills (1990–92); and Rich, a tackle/guard who played for the New York Giants (1982–83), Kansas City Chiefs (1983–92), and New England Patriots (1993).

BREAKAWAY RUNS

(25 questions, 30 yards each)

1. Who kicked the game-winning field goal for the AFC in its 23–20 overtime win over the NFC in the 1993 Pro Bowl?

2. Name either of the teams current Tampa Bay Buccaneers coach Tony Dungy played for during his three-year NFL career (1977–79).

3. The Pro Football Hall of Fame Class of 1991 consists of five men: one affiliated with the New England Patriots; one with the Houston Oilers and New Orleans Saints; one with the Chicago Bears and Washington Redskins; one with the Kansas City Chiefs, Green Bay Packers, and Minnesota Vikings; and one with the Los Angeles Rams and Dallas Cowboys. Name any of the five.

4. Name the tight end who scored the Philadelphia Eagles' lone touchdown in their 27–10 loss to the Oakland Raiders in Super Bowl XV.

5. Jimmy Johnson's coaching debut with the Miami Dolphins in 1996 resulted in a victory over what AFC East rival?

6. Quarterback Jim Everett, who played from his rookie season of 1986 through '93 with the Los Angeles

Rams, wasn't drafted by the Rams. Which AFC Central team drafted him?

7. Name the former Baltimore Colts star who holds the record for consecutive games with at least one touchdown scored, with 18.

8. Three-time Pro Bowl running back Chris Warren played his freshman and sophomore seasons of college football at the University of Virginia—as a defensive back—before transferring in 1988 to what in-state Division III school: Emory & Henry College, Ferrum College, Randolph-Macon College, or Washington and Lee University?

9. What was the first expansion franchise awarded by the AFL? (Hint: It happened in 1965.)

10. What NFL team has the worst all-time winning percentage on opening day?

11. Which AFC quarterback was named the NFL's most valuable player for the 1988 season?

12. Who led the New York Giants in receptions in their Super Bowl championship season of 1986?

13. Only four special-teams players ever have been named most valuable player of the Pro Bowl. Name any one of them.

14. An AFC player and an NFC player finished tied for the NFL lead in 1996 with nine interceptions. Name either one of them.

15. Who holds the New York Jets' career interceptions record? (Hint: He played defensive back for the team from 1963 to 1969.)

16. By what nickname was Hall of Fame coach Earle Neale, who led the Philadelphia Eagles to back-to-back NFL championships in 1948 and '49, known?

17. How many rushing yards did then-All-Pro Dallas Cowboys backfield mates Emmitt Smith and Daryl Johnston combine for in 1996 (each started 15 games): 1,252; 1,452; 1,652; or 1,852?

18. What AFC Central team from 1981 to 1984 set the all-time NFL record for consecutive road losses, with 23?

19. Name the former offensive lineman who holds the NFL record for the most seasons played with one team.

20. What is Washington Redskins coach Norv Turner's full first name (spelled correctly)?

21. What team did the Denver Broncos defeat 20–17 in the 1977 AFC Championship Game to advance to Super Bowl XII?

22. San Diego Chargers coach Kevin Gilbride previously served two-season stints as offensive coordinator with what two NFL teams?

23. Who holds the San Diego Chargers' career rushing record? (Hint: He played for the team from 1960 to 1967.)

24. What AFL team selected Penn State quarterback Richie Lucas in 1960 with its first-ever draft pick?

25. Where did Hall of Fame linebacker Dick Butkus play in college?

ANSWERS

1. Nick Lowery, then of the Kansas City Chiefs, in the last of his three Pro Bowls.

2. The teams: the Pittsburgh Steelers and the San Francisco 49ers. Dungy, a defensive back, played for the Steelers in 1977 and '78 and the 49ers in '79.

3. The five, in order: guard John Hannah, running back Earl Campbell, guard/defensive tackle Stan Jones, kicker Jan Stenerud, and team president/general manager Tex Schramm.

4. Keith Krepfle, on an eight-yard pass from Ron Jaworski with a minute gone in the fourth quarter.

5. The New England Patriots, by a score of 24–10.

6. The Houston Oilers (with the number three overall pick), who then traded his rights to the Rams for a pair of players and three draft picks.

7. Lenny Moore, whose streak started late in the 1963 season and ended early in the '65 season.

8. Ferrum College.

9. The Miami Dolphins, who began play in 1966, participated in the first AFL-NFL interleague game (vs. Atlanta) in '67, began play in the NFL in '70 after the leagues' merger, and had their first Super Bowl championship season by '72.

10. The New Orleans Saints, who were 7–24–0 (.226) through 1997.

11. Boomer Esiason of the Cincinnati Bengals, who led the league with a 97.4 passer rating and threw 28 touchdown passes that season.

12. Tight end Mark Bavaro, with 66.

13. The four: the Kansas City Chiefs' Jan Stenerud in 1972 (four field goals); the Miami Dolphins' Garo Yepremian in '74 (five field goals, including a game-winning 42-yarder with 21 seconds remaining); the Detroit Lions' Eddie Murray in '81 (four field goals); and the Buffalo Bills' Steve Tasker in '93 (four special-teams tackles, a forced fumble, and a blocked field goal).

14. The Denver Broncos' Tyrone Braxton and the St. Louis Rams' Keith Lyle.

15. Bill Baird, with 34.

16. "Greasy."

17. They combined for only 1,252 yards. Smith's 1,204 was his lowest total since his rookie season of 1990, and Johnston's 48 was his lowest total since he became a full-time starter in 1991.

18. The Houston Oilers, who finally broke the streak November 11, 1984, with a 17–16 win at the Kansas City Chiefs.
19. Jackie Slater, who played offensive tackle for 20 seasons (1976–95) in the Rams organization (the first 19 in Los Angeles and the last one in St. Louis).
20. Norval.
21. The Oakland Raiders.
22. The Houston Oilers (1993–94) and Jacksonville Jaguars (1995–96).
23. Paul Lowe, with 4,963 yards.
24. The Buffalo Bills. Lucas didn't exactly light the pro game on fire; he spent two seasons with the Bills, first as a quarterback, then as a halfback, and finally as a defensive back, before calling it a career.
25. The University of Illinois.

BOMBS AWAY

(25 questions, 50 yards each)

1. Before launching his career in the NFL, former San Francisco 49ers head coach George Seifert served in the same capacity at two different colleges. Name both.
2. Name all four NFL teams, in order, that quarterback Mike Tomczak has played for.
3. Hall of Fame wide receiver Fred Biletnikoff, who starred for the Oakland Raiders from 1965 to 1978, played one season (1980) in the Canadian Football League. With what CFL team did he play?
4. The Pro Football Hall of Fame Class of 1989 consists of four men: two affiliated with the Pittsburgh Steelers; one with the Oakland Raiders; and one with the Green Bay Packers. Name any of the four.
5. Hall-of-Famer George Blanda owns the NFL record for most games played, with 340. Who's second on the list, with 282?
6. Name any five of the six NFL teams wide receiver Andre Rison has played for.
7. Marcus Allen holds the Oakland Raiders' record for touchdowns in a season, with 18. Name the two players who stand right behind him, with 16. (Hint:

They accomplished the feat in 1963 and '75, respectively.)

8. On March 23, 1959, in one of the biggest trades in NFL history, the Chicago Cardinals dealt halfback Ollie Matson to the Los Angeles Rams for seven active players, one draft pick, and one player to be named. Name any one of the seven active players L.A. gave up.

9. At what university did Dick Vermeil coach for two seasons before being hired in 1976 to coach the Philadelphia Eagles?

10. In what city was New England Patriots quarterback Drew Bledsoe born?

11. Future Hall of Fame quarterback Warren Moon actually has a different first name (Warren is his middle name). What is it?

12. Quarterback Jeff Hostetler is the son-in-law of what longtime college football coach?

13. Name the Miami Dolphins player who had four interceptions in a "Monday Night Football" game on December 3, 1973.

14. Two teams share the NFC record for consecutive road losses, with 19. One is the Tampa Bay Buccaneers, who did it from 1983 to 1985. Name the other team. (Hint: It did it from 1988 to 1991.)

15. Where did Hall of Fame cornerback Mel Blount play in college?

16. What is the NFL team record for most punts returned for touchdowns in a season?

17. What AFC team in the 1980s became the first NFL team ever to win three road games in one postseason?

18. In what city was Detroit Lions running back Barry Sanders born?

19. Before Bill Walsh signed on to coach the San Francisco 49ers in 1979, the team was coached by two

men—one who resigned after nine games, the other his replacement—in '78. Name both men.

20. The Buffalo Bills had a different rushing leader in each of the three seasons before Thurman Thomas's rookie season of 1988. Name any two of them.

21. Name the Denver Broncos player who led all AFL and NFL punters in average in both 1966 and '67. (Hint: His first name is Bob.)

22. Name either of the teams involved in the first regular-season game in AFL history, a 13–10 affair September 9, 1960.

23. Name the Hall-of-Famer who was the first player in NFL history to rush for 200 yards in a game. (Hint: He did it in 1933.)

24. What was the name of the NFL team in Staten Island, New York, from 1929 to 1932?

25. What is the only NFL team with a logo on only one side of its helmets?

ANSWERS

1. Seifert led Westminster College—the one in Utah, not the one in Missouri or the one in Pennsylvania—in 1965, and Cornell in 1975 and '76.

2. Tomczak played for the Chicago Bears from 1985 to 1990, the Green Bay Packers in '91, and the Cleveland Browns in '92, before settling in with the Pittsburgh Steelers in '93.

3. The Montreal Alouettes.

4. The four, in order: cornerback Mel Blount and quarterback Terry Bradshaw, tackle Art Shell, and safety Willie Wood.

5. Jim Marshall, another Hall-of-Famer, who played as

a rookie with the Cleveland Browns in 1960 before anchoring the Minnesota Vikings' defensive line from 1961 to 1979.

6. The six: the Indianapolis Colts (1989), Atlanta Falcons (1990–94), Cleveland Browns ('95), Jacksonville Jaguars ('96), Green Bay Packers ('96), and Kansas City Chiefs.

7. Wide receiver Art Powell and running back Pete Banaszak.

8. Tackle Frank Fuller, defensive end Glenn Holtzman, tackle Ken Panfil, defensive tackle Art Hauser, end John Tracy, fullback Larry Hickman, and halfback Don Brown.

9. UCLA, where Vermeil was 14–5–3 and led the Bruins to a Rose Bowl win after the 1975 season.

10. Walla Walla, Washington.

11. Harold.

12. West Virginia's Don Nehlen.

13. Dick Anderson—and the Dolphins, who beat the Pittsburgh Steelers 30–26 that night, needed every one of them.

14. The Atlanta Falcons, who finally broke the streak September 8, 1991, with a 13–10 victory at the San Diego Chargers.

15. Southern University.

16. Five, by the 1959 Chicago Cardinals. The touchdowns were scored by four different players; only Billy Stacy had two.

17. The New England Patriots, who in 1985 won an AFC wild-card game at the New York Jets 26–14, a divisional playoff game at the Los Angeles Raiders 27–20, and the conference championship game at the Miami Dolphins 31–14.

18. Wichita.

19. Pete McCulley, who went 1–8 before stepping down, and Fred O'Connor, an "interim coach" who went

1–6 over the final seven games of the season.
20. The three: Greg Bell in 1985 with 883 yards, Robb Riddick in '86 with 632, and Ronnie Harmon in '87 with 485.
21. Bob Scarpitto, with a 45.8-yard average (on 76 punts) in 1966 and a 44.9-yard average (105) in '67.
22. The Denver Broncos, who won, and the Boston Patriots. (''New England Patriots'' is not an acceptable answer.)
23. Cliff Battles.
24. The Staten Island Stapletons, whose best season was 1930 (5–5–2).
25. The Pittsburgh Steelers.

FIELD GOALS

INSIDE THE 20

(25 questions)

1. True or false: By the end of the 1997 season, both the Carolina Panthers and the Jacksonville Jaguars had appeared at least once on "Monday Night Football."
2. True or false: Dallas Cowboys quarterback Troy Aikman, who was drafted by the team out of UCLA, began his college career at the University of Oklahoma.
3. What team did the New England Patriots defeat 20–6 at home in the 1996 AFC Championship Game?
4. By what nickname was former Chicago Bears star defensive tackle William Perry known?
5. With what team did star defensive lineman Chester McGlockton play the first six seasons of his NFL career (1992–97) before signing as a free agent with the Kansas City Chiefs in 1998?
6. Which one of the following former Green Bay Packers draftees was not a first-round pick: running back

Edgar Bennett, offensive tackle Tony Mandarich, or wide receiver Sterling Sharpe?

7. What team did the San Diego Chargers defeat 17–13 on the road in the 1994 AFC Championship Game?

8. True or false: Green Bay Packers quarterback Brett Favre played in college at Penn State.

9. How high above the field must the top facing of a crossbar be: 10 feet or 10 yards?

10. About whom was the book *Bo Knows Bo: The Autobiography of a Ballplayer* written?

11. Who is the Pittsburgh Steelers' all-time leader in passing yards and touchdown passes?

12. Who is the New York Jets' all-time leader in passing yards and touchdown passes?

13. What team did the San Francisco 49ers defeat 38–28 at home in the 1994 NFC Championship Game?

14. Has San Francisco 49ers quarterback Steve Young ever rushed for at least 100 yards in an NFL game?

15. Name the wide receiver with the initials "C.C." who caught 417 passes for the Cincinnati Bengals from 1981 to 1988.

16. Which one of the following former Denver Broncos draftees was not a first-round pick: running back Terrell Davis, quarterback John Elway, or linebacker Randy Gradishar?

17. By what nickname was Hall of Fame running back Walter Payton known: "Paydirt," "Smiley," "Sweetness," or "Walter Wonder"?

18. Which one of the following former Tampa Bay Buccaneers draftees was not a first-round pick: defensive end Chidi Ahanotu, defensive end Lee Roy Selmon, or quarterback Vinny Testaverde?

19. True or false: San Francisco 49ers wide receiver Jerry Rice is a former first-round draft pick.

20. True or false: Carolina Panthers running back Tshi-manga Biakabutuka played in college at Georgia Tech.

21. What jersey number does Cincinnati Bengals quarterback Jeff Blake wear: number 8 or number 16?

22. Which one of the following former Pittsburgh Steelers draftees was not a first-round pick: quarterback Bubby Brister, wide receiver Lynn Swann, or cornerback Rod Woodson?

23. Name the only player whose jersey number has been retired by the Tampa Bay Buccaneers.

24. What jersey number does Tampa Bay Buccaneers quarterback Trent Dilfer wear: number 1 or number 12?

25. By what nickname was former Oakland Raiders and Kansas City Chiefs star defensive back Fred Williamson known: "Drop Dead," "the Hammer," "the Master of Disaster," or "the Tiger"?

20–29 YARDS
(25 questions)

1. What jersey number does Green Bay Packers wide receiver Robert Brooks wear: number 83 or number 87?

2. Wide receiver Yancey Thigpen spent a low-profile rookie season of 1991 with the San Diego Chargers, then flourished with his next team before signing as a free agent with the Tennessee Oilers in '98. With what team did he play from 1992 to 1997?

3. Which one of the following former Philadelphia Eagles draftees was not a first-round pick: defensive

tackle Andy Harmon, tight end Keith Jackson, or defensive end Mike Mamula?

4. True or false: The New England Patriots once played their home games in Fenway Park.

5. True or false: San Francisco 49ers wide receiver J.J. Stokes played in college at the University of Florida.

6. Name the NFL's all-time leader in seasons played, with 26.

7. True or false: Tampa Bay Buccaneers quarterback Trent Dilfer played in college at Fresno State.

8. Which one of the following former Miami Dolphins draftees was not a first-round pick: defensive end A.J. Duhe, quarterback Bob Griese, or wide receiver Mark Clayton?

9. In what facility did the Chicago Bears play the vast majority of their home games before moving into their current facility in 1971?

10. In what round did the Pittsburgh Steelers draft quarterback Kordell Stewart in 1995: the second or the seventh?

11. Which one of the following former New Orleans Saints draftees was not a first-round pick: quarterback Archie Manning, wide receiver Eric Martin, or cornerback Alex Molden?

12. Who is considered the originator of the Oakland Raiders motto, ''Just win, baby''?

13. Which one of the following former Arizona Cardinals draftees was not a first-round pick: quarterback Stoney Case, defensive end Simeon Rice, or defensive end Andre Wadsworth?

14. Oakland Raiders quarterback Jeff George finished his college career at Illinois, but he spent his freshman year at another Big Ten school. From which Hoosier State school did the Indianapolis native transfer to Illinois: Indiana or Purdue?

15. What team did the New York Giants defeat 49–3 at home in the 1986 NFC divisional playoffs, for the fourth-largest margin of victory in NFL postseason history: the San Francisco 49ers or the Tampa Bay Buccaneers?

16. True or false: No player ever has scored more than three touchdowns in a "Monday Night Football" game.

17. How many yards is an offense penalized on an offensive pass interference call?

18. What all-time NFL great is known as the "Minister of Defense"?

19. Which one of the following former Chicago Bears draftees was not a first-round pick: wide receiver Curtis Conway, defensive end Richard Dent, or defensive tackle William Perry?

20. About whom is the book entitled *Tex: The Man Who Built the Dallas Cowboys*?

21. Who passed for more yards and touchdowns than anyone else in Cleveland Browns history? (Hint: He played with the team from 1974 to 1983.)

22. What jersey number does Miami Dolphins running back Karim Abdul-Jabbar wear: number 33 or number 48? (Hint: Think of his name.)

23. What team did the Buffalo Bills defeat 41–38 in overtime at home in the 1992 AFC wild-card playoffs—after trailing 35–3 in the third quarter of that game?

24. What jersey number does Seattle Seahawks wide receiver Joey Galloway wear: number 19 or number 84?

25. With what team did star fullback William Floyd play the first four seasons of his NFL career (1994–97) before signing as a free agent with the Carolina Panthers in 1998?

30–39 YARDS
(25 questions)

1. How much did it cost Pittsburgh's Art Rooney in 1933 to purchase an NFL franchise: $2,500; $25,000; or $250,000?

2. In 1997 Detroit Lions running back Barry Sanders set the all-time NFL record for 100-yard rushing games in a season, with how many: 11 or 14?

3. Which one of the following former Kansas City Chiefs draftees was not a first-round pick: cornerback Dale Carter, running back Greg Hill, or guard Will Shields?

4. True or false: Quarterback Rich Gannon never has started 10 or more games in a single NFL season.

5. What AFC West team did the Buffalo Bills defeat 10–7 at home in the 1991 AFC Championship Game?

6. True or false: No quarterback ever has thrown for 400 or more yards in an NFL game on Thanksgiving Day.

7. Name the last NFL player to rush for at least 2,000 yards in a single regular season.

8. What team did the Oakland Raiders defeat 37–31 on a 10-yard Ken Stabler-to-Dave Casper pass in overtime on the road in the 1977 AFC divisional playoffs: the Baltimore Colts or the Kansas City Chiefs?

9. What AFC East team led the NFL in fewest penalties committed every season from 1976 to 1984?

10. In 1975, what appropriately named team became the first in the NFL to use the ''shotgun'' formation in most passing situations?

11. True or false: NFL officials once blew horns to signal penalties.

12. Which one of the following former San Francisco 49ers draftees was not a first-round pick: defensive back Ronnie Lott, defensive tackle Bryant Young, or linebacker Lee Woodall?

13. True or false: No NFL quarterback passed for at least 4,000 yards in 1997.

14. In what year did the NFL rule the five interior offensive linemen—the center, two guards, and two tackles—ineligible to catch a forward pass: 1931, 1951, or 1971?

15. What AFC Central team did the Kansas City Chiefs defeat 27–24 on a 32-yard Nick Lowery field goal in overtime at home in the 1993 AFC wild-card play-offs?

16. True or false: Quarterback Warren Moon never has rushed for at least 100 yards in an NFL game.

17. True or false: Former San Francisco 49ers four-time Pro Bowler Brent Jones was originally drafted by the Pittsburgh Steelers.

18. Take three guesses to come up with either of the two players in NFL history who scored at least 10 touchdowns in each of their first five seasons.

19. Which one of the following three jobs has Al Davis never held: AFL commissioner, "Monday Night Football" commentator, or San Diego Chargers assistant coach?

20. Which one of the following former Detroit Lions draftees was not a first-round pick: defensive end Al "Bubba" Baker, running back Billy Sims, or cornerback Bryant Westbrook?

21. Which of the following Hall-of-Fame ball-carriers had the shortest career: Frank Gifford, Marion Motley, or Gale Sayers?

22. Which one of the following former Washington Redskins also played two seasons of major league baseball with the Pittsburgh Pirates: Vic Janowicz, John Riggins, or Doug Williams?

23. What position did Hall-of-Famer Frank Gatski—who played for the Cleveland Browns (1946–56) and Detroit Lions ('57)—play: center or defensive end?

24. Take two guesses to name the only quarterback in NFL history (through 1997) to complete 4,000 passes in his career.

25. Through the 1997 season, there had been 31 single-season 4,000-yard passing performances in NFL history. Did quarterbacks throw for at least 30 touchdowns in a majority of those instances?

40–49 YARDS
(25 questions)

1. What two teams played in the "Fog Bowl" on December 31, 1988?

2. What team drafted University of Louisville quarterback Johnny Unitas in 1955: the Baltimore Colts, Chicago Bears, or Pittsburgh Steelers?

3. With what team did quarterback Joe Namath play in 1977, the final year of his NFL career: the Los Angeles Rams, New York Jets, or San Diego Chargers?

4. What AFC West team did the Cincinnati Bengals defeat 27–7 at home—with the temperature at 9 degrees below zero and the wind at 35 miles an hour, creating a wind-chill factor of minus-59—in the 1981 AFC Championship Game?

5. What AFC East team did the Cleveland Browns defeat 23–20 on a 27-yard Mark Moseley field goal in overtime at home in the 1986 AFC divisional play-offs?

6. Which one of the following former Minnesota Vikings draftees was not a first-round pick: running

back Chuck Foreman, quarterback Brad Johnson, or wide receiver Randy Moss?

7. Entering the 1998 season, what team had played an all-time NFL-record 322 consecutive regular-season games without being shut out: the Atlanta Falcons, Cincinnati Bengals, or San Francisco 49ers?

8. What New Orleans Saints player in 1996 and '95 recorded the highest and second-highest single-season individual totals, respectively, for kickoff returns in NFL history?

9. What AFC Central team did the Miami Dolphins defeat 45–28 at home in the 1984 AFC Championship Game?

10. What AFC West team did the Houston Oilers defeat 23–20 on a 42-yard Tony Zendejas field goal in overtime at home in the 1987 AFC wild-card playoffs?

11. Hall-of-Famer George Musso was an All-NFL tackle in 1935 and an All-NFL guard in '37, the first league player ever to be named All-NFL at two different positions. What team did he play for?

12. What NFC East team did the Los Angeles Rams defeat 19–13 on a 30-yard Jim Everett-to-Flipper Anderson pass in overtime on the road in the 1989 NFC divisional playoffs?

13. In what facility did the San Francisco 49ers play from their inception in 1946 through '70?

14. By what nickname was Detroit Lions fullback Tommy Vardell known during his college days at Stanford?

15. What AFC East team did the Cincinnati Bengals defeat 21–10 at home in the 1988 AFC Championship Game?

16. The first commissioner of the AFL, Joe Foss, was a highly decorated World War II fighter pilot and the governor of what state: Alabama or South Dakota?

17. Name the left-handed quarterback who led all NFL

QBs in passing yards and rushing yards in 1996 to become the first player since Johnny Unitas in 1963 to pull off that doubly impressive accomplishment.

18. Who is the Denver Broncos' all-time leader in receptions and receiving yards? (Hint: He never played with John Elway.)

19. With what team did legendary coach Tom Landry star as a defensive back/punter for his entire six-year NFL career (1950–55): the Detroit Lions, Green Bay Packers, or New York Giants?

20. Who is the Arizona Cardinals' all-time leader in receptions and receiving yards? (Hint: He played with the team only when it was in St. Louis.)

21. Who was the first quarterback to throw at least 40 touchdown passes in one NFL season: the Pittsburgh Steelers' Terry Bradshaw, the Miami Dolphins' Dan Marino, the Oakland Raiders' Ken Stabler, or the Minnesota Vikings' Fran Tarkenton?

22. How many men played in all 10 seasons of the AFL's existence (1960–69): none, one, or 19?

23. What jersey number does Green Bay Packers wide receiver Antonio Freeman wear?

24. How many Super Bowl winners have had a losing record the season before their championship campaign: one or five?

25. Who is the Philadelphia Eagles' all-time leader in receptions and receiving yards?

50–55 YARDS
(25 questions)

1. What is the most yards Miami Dolphins quarterback Dan Marino ever has rushed for in an NFL game: 18, 38, 58, or 78?

2. What Los Angeles Raiders player returned an interception an all-time "Monday Night Football"-high 102 yards for his team's only score in a 20–7 loss at the Miami Dolphins in 1992?

3. What NFC West team did the Atlanta Falcons defeat 27–20 on the road in the 1991 NFC wild-card playoffs?

4. What AFC Central team did the Denver Broncos defeat 24–23 at home in the 1989 AFC divisional playoffs?

5. Two current NFC wide receivers share the all-time "Monday Night Football" record for receptions in a game, with 14. Name both of them.

6. What NFC Central team did the San Francisco 49ers defeat 34–9 at home in the 1988 NFC divisional playoffs?

7. In 1992 the Pittsburgh Steelers hired Kansas City Chiefs defensive coordinator Bill Cowher to be their head coach. For which AFC Central team was Cowher an assistant before moving to the Chiefs?

8. What NFC East team did the San Francisco 49ers defeat 28–10 at home in the 1990 NFC divisional playoffs?

9. What AFC West team did the Kansas City Chiefs defeat 10–6 at home in the 1991 AFC wild-card playoffs?

10. What NFC Central team did the Washington Redskins defeat 24–7 on the road in the 1992 NFC wild-card playoffs?

11. How wide is the in-bounds portion of an NFL field: 99 feet (33 yards), 120 feet, 150 feet, or 160 feet?

12. Which two of the following former quarterbacks share the career record for most interceptions thrown in the Super Bowl, with seven: Terry Bradshaw, Jim Kelly, Craig Morton, and Roger Staubach?

13. What NFC East team did the Washington Redskins

defeat 20–6 on the road in the 1990 NFC wild-card playoffs?

14. What AFC Central team did the Buffalo Bills defeat 17–10 at home in the 1988 AFC divisional playoffs?

15. Who is the Chicago Bears' all-time leader in passing yards and touchdown passes?

16. What team did the Carolina Panthers defeat 26–15 at home in their sixth game of the 1995 season for their first regular-season win ever: the Chicago Bears, Denver Broncos, New York Jets, or San Francisco 49ers?

17. What NFC East team did the Los Angeles Rams defeat 21–7 on the road in the 1989 NFC wild-card playoffs?

18. What AFC East team did the Buffalo Bills defeat 44–34 at home in the 1990 AFC divisional playoffs?

19. Name the former Kansas City Chiefs and San Diego Chargers running back who was the only player ever to rush for 1,000 yards in a season in both the AFL and the NFL.

20. What jersey number does Buffalo Bills running back Antowain Smith wear?

21. What AFC West team did the Miami Dolphins defeat 17–16 at home in the 1990 AFC wild-card playoffs?

22. What AFC Central team did the Houston Oilers defeat 24–23 at home in the 1988 AFC wild-card playoffs?

23. Name the only player whose jersey number has been retired by the Cincinnati Bengals.

24. Of the following current NFL defensive tackles, who was a state wrestling champion in high school: Jim Flanigan, Andy Harmon, Tony Siragusa, or Chris Zorich?

25. The Dallas Cowboys have lost three Super Bowls—all in what city?

ANSWERS

Inside the 20

1. True. Although neither team played on Monday night in 1995 or '96, their first two seasons in the league, the Panthers appeared twice and the Jaguars once on "MNF" in '97.
2. True. Aikman played at Oklahoma in 1984 and '85, then transferred to UCLA, where he starred in '87 and '88.
3. The Jacksonville Jaguars.
4. "Refrigerator."
5. The Oakland Raiders (who were in Los Angeles through the 1994 season), with whom he started 80 regular-season games, had 39.5 sacks, and played in four Pro Bowls.
6. Bennett, who was selected out of Florida State in the fourth round in 1992.
7. The Pittsburgh Steelers.
8. False. Favre played at Southern Mississippi, where he set school records for passing yards (8,193), pass attempts (1,234), completions (656), and touchdown passes (55).
9. Ten feet.
10. Beauregard Wojciechowski—not really, of course. It was Bo Jackson.
11. Terry Bradshaw, who threw for 27,989 yards and 212 touchdowns with the team from 1970 to 1983.
12. Joe Namath, who threw for 27,057 yards and 170 touchdowns with the team from 1965 to 1976.
13. The Dallas Cowboys.
14. Young has done it once, in a 13–10 loss at home to the New Orleans Saints in 1990, when he carried eight times for 102 yards.

15. Cris Collinsworth.
16. Davis, who was selected out of the University of Georgia in the sixth round in 1995.
17. "Sweetness."
18. Ahanotu, who was selected out of the University of California in the sixth round in 1993.
19. True. Rice was drafted number 16 overall by the 49ers in 1985. That same year, the Birmingham Stallions of the USFL drafted Rice number one overall, but the player opted for the more-established league.
20. False. Biakabutuka played at the University of Michigan, where he set a school rushing record with 1,818 yards as a junior, then skipped his senior season to enter the NFL draft..
21. Number 8.
22. Brister, who was selected out of Northeast Louisiana in the third round in 1986.
23. Lee Roy Selmon (number 63).
24. Number 12.
25. "The Hammer."

20–29 yards
1. Number 87.
2. The Pittsburgh Steelers, with whom he had 222 receptions for 3,651 yards and 21 touchdowns, and played in two Pro Bowls.
3. Harmon, who was selected out of Kent State in the sixth round in 1991.
4. True. They played there from 1963 to 1968, back when they were known as the Boston Patriots.
5. False. Stokes played at UCLA, where he concluded his four-year career as the school's all-time leader in receptions (154), receiving yards (2,469), and touchdown receptions (28).
6. George Blanda, who broke into the league in 1949 with the Chicago Bears and retired in '75 as an Oak-

land Raider; his 26 years of service is five better than
Earl Morrall's next-longest total of 21 seasons.

7. True. He threw for 6,944 yards and 51 touchdowns
at the school before skipping his senior season to
enter the NFL draft.

8. Clayton, who was selected out of Louisville in the
eighth round in 1983.

9. Wrigley Field.

10. Stewart, who played in college at the University of
Colorado, was drafted in the second round (number
60 overall).

11. Martin, who was selected out of Louisiana State in
the seventh round in 1985.

12. Al Davis.

13. Case, who was selected out of the University of New
Mexico in the third round in 1995.

14. True. George played at Purdue as a freshman before
transferring to the University of Illinois.

15. San Francisco.

16. False. Five players have scored four touchdowns in
one "MNF" game: the New York Giants' Ron Johnson, in a 27–12 win at the Philadelphia Eagles in
1972; the Houston Oilers' Earl Campbell, in a 35–30
win at home against the Miami Dolphins in '78; the
Los Angeles Raiders' Marcus Allen, in a 33–30 win
at home against the San Diego Chargers in '84; the
Indianapolis Colts' Eric Dickerson, in a 55–23 win
at home against the Denver Broncos in '88; and the
Dallas Cowboys' Emmitt Smith, in a 35–0 win at the
Giants in '95.

17. Ten.

18. Reggie White, who is both an ordained minister and
a 12–time Pro Bowl defensive end.

19. Dent, who was selected out of Tennessee State in the
eighth round in 1983.

20. Tex Schramm, the Dallas Cowboys' first general

manager and the man widely credited with engineering the "America's Team" image.

21. Brian Sipe, with 23,713 yards and 154 touchdowns.
22. Number 33—just like a certain former basketball player we know named Kareem Abdul-Jabbar.
23. The Houston Oilers, in the biggest comeback in NFL history (regular season or playoffs).
24. Number 84.
25. The San Francisco 49ers, with whom the punishing blocker started 42 regular-season games, had 13 rushing touchdowns, and caught 129 passes for three more TDs.

30–39 yards

1. It cost Rooney $2,500—as legend has it, almost precisely what the former semipro football player had won at the racetrack a short time before the purchase.
2. Fourteen. Sanders broke by two games the record that was co-held by Eric Dickerson (Los Angeles Rams, 1984) and Barry Foster (Pittsburgh Steelers, 1992).
3. Shields, who was selected out of the University of Nebraska in the third round in 1993.
4. False. Gannon has done it three times, all when he was with the Minnesota Vikings; he started 12 games in 1990, 11 in '91, and 12 more in '92, his last season in Minnesota.
5. The Denver Broncos.
6. False. It's been done by one player, the Detroit Lions' Scott Mitchell, who threw for 410 yards in a 44–38 win at home over the Minnesota Vikings in 1995.
7. Barry Sanders of the Detroit Lions, who rushed for 2,053 yards in 1997, the second-highest total in NFL history.
8. The Baltimore Colts.

9. The Miami Dolphins.
10. The Dallas Cowboys. However, it should be noted that the shotgun was first conceived and implemented in an NFL game by San Francisco 49ers coach Red Kickey back in 1960.
11. True. Horns were used to indicate infractions before the penalty flag was introduced in 1948. (Of course, some would argue that losing the horns hasn't stopped many officials from "blowing calls.")
12. Woodall, who was selected out of West Chester (Pennsylvania) in the sixth round in 1994.
13. True. The leader in passing yardage was the Oakland Raiders' Jeff George, with 3,917. It was the first time since 1987 that no NFL quarterback topped the 4,000-yard mark.
14. It was 1951.
15. The Pittsburgh Steelers.
16. True. Moon's career high is 47 yards, set in 1985 when his Houston Oilers lost 16–13 at the Washington Redskins.
17. True. Jones, who was with the 49ers from 1987 to 1997—and whose father, Mike Jones, was drafted by both the AFL Oakland Raiders and the NFL Steelers in 1961 but never made it as a pro—was drafted out of Santa Clara by the Steelers in '86. He suffered a neck injury in training camp as a rookie, was placed on injured reserve and then waived, and was picked up by the 49ers after the '86 regular season.
18. The two: Jim Brown of the Cleveland Browns, whose first five seasons (1957–61) produced 10, 18, 14, 11, and 10 touchdowns; and Emmitt Smith of the Dallas Cowboys, whose first five seasons (1990–94) produced 11, 13, 19, 10, and 22 TDs.
19. "Monday Night Football" commentator. Davis was the Chargers' offensive ends coach before the Oakland Raiders hired him in 1963 to be their coach and

general manager, and he served a brief stint in '66 as AFL commissioner before returning to the Raiders later that year as managing general partner.

20. Baker, who was selected out of Colorado State in the second round in 1978.

21. Sayers, who played for only seven seasons (1965–71), all with the Chicago Bears. Gifford played 12 seasons (1952–60, 1962–64), all with the New York Giants; Motley played nine seasons: eight (1946–53) with the Cleveland Browns and one ('55) with the Pittsburgh Steelers.

22. Janowicz, who played catcher and third base with the Pirates in 1953 and '54, and halfback with the Redskins in '54 and '55.

23. Center.

24. Dan Marino of the Miami Dolphins, who threw his 4,000th completion in 1996 and entered the '98 season with 4,453.

25. No. Quarterbacks threw for at least 30 touchdowns in only 13 of the 31 4,000-yard seasons; they averaged 28.7 TDs in those campaigns.

40–49 yards

1. The Chicago Bears and Philadelphia Eagles. In an NFC divisional playoff game at Chicago's Soldier Field, the Bears beat the Eagles 20–12 in fog so thick the action was barely visible even on television.

2. The Steelers, who wound up cutting Unitas, allowing the Colts to pick him up on waivers in 1956.

3. The Rams, with whom Namath played in four games and completed 50 of 107 passes for 606 yards and three touchdowns, with five interceptions.

4. The San Diego Chargers.

5. The New York Jets.

6. Johnson, who was selected out of Florida State in the ninth round in 1992.

7. The 49ers, whose last scoring-free outing had come in a 7–0 loss at home to Atlanta in 1977.

8. Tyrone Hughes, who returned 70 kickoffs for 1,791 yards (25.6 average) in 1996 and 66 kickoffs for 1,617 yards (24.5) in '95.

9. The Pittsburgh Steelers.

10. The Seattle Seahawks.

11. The Chicago Bears, from 1933 to 1944.

12. The New York Giants.

13. Kezar Stadium.

14. "Touchdown Tommy," for setting a school career record with 37 touchdowns, including 20 in his senior season. Of course, Vardell didn't exactly live up to that nickname with the team that drafted him, the Cleveland Browns—he scored all of five TDs in 40 games with the team from 1992 to 1995.

15. The Buffalo Bills.

16. South Dakota.

17. Mark Brunell of the Jacksonville Jaguars, who had 4,367 yards passing and 396 yards rushing. Unfortunately, not everything worked out well for Brunell that season—he also was sacked an NFL-high 50 times.

18. Lionel Taylor, with 543 catches for 6,872 yards from 1960 to 1966.

19. The Giants, with whom Landry amassed career totals of 31 interceptions for 360 yards and three touchdowns, and 338 punts for 13,651 yards (a 40.4-yard average).

20. Roy Green, with 522 catches for 8,497 yards from 1979–90.

21. Marino, who threw for 48 touchdowns in 1984. Marino, who also threw for 44 scores in '86, remains the only NFL quarterback ever to eclipse the 40-TD mark in a season.

22. Nineteen.

23. Number 86.
24. One: the San Francisco 49ers, who were 6–10 in 1980 before rebounding in '81 to win it all.
25. Harold Carmichael, with 589 catches for 8,978 yards from 1971–83.

50–55 yards
1. Eighteen—15 of which came on one carry—in a 17–6 loss at the New England Patriots in 1983, his rookie season.
2. Eddie Anderson, a safety. As long as his return was, it was still one yard short of the NFL record, which is shared by two more safeties: the San Diego Chargers' Vencie Glenn, who did it in 1987, and the Miami Dolphins' Louis Oliver, who did it in '92.
3. The New Orleans Saints.
4. The Pittsburgh Steelers.
5. Herman Moore of the Detroit Lions, who set the mark in a 27–7 win at home over the Chicago Bears in 1995, and Jerry Rice of the San Francisco 49ers, who matched it later that season in a 37–30 win at home over the Minnesota Vikings.
6. The Minnesota Vikings.
7. The Cleveland Browns, for whom Cowher was special-teams coach in 1985 and '86 and defensive backs coach in 1987 and '88.
8. The Washington Redskins.
9. The Los Angeles Raiders.
10. The Minnesota Vikings.
11. 160 feet.
12. Kelly and Morton. The Buffalo Bills' Kelly, who played in four Super Bowls, threw four interceptions in one of the games and one INT in each of the other three; Morton was picked off four times in the one Super Bowl he played with the Denver Broncos, and three times in the one title game he played with the

Dallas Cowboys. Both the Pittsburgh Steelers' Bradshaw and Dallas' Staubach were intercepted four
times in Super Bowls.

13. The Philadelphia Eagles.

14. The Houston Oilers.

15. Sid Luckman, who threw for 14,686 yards and 137
    touchdowns from 1939 to 1950.

16. The New York Jets.

17. The Philadelphia Eagles.

18. The Miami Dolphins.

19. Mike Garrett, with 1,087 yards in 1967 for the AFL
    Chiefs and 1,031 in '72 for the NFL Chargers.

20. Number 26.

21. The Kansas City Chiefs.

22. The Cleveland Browns.

23. Bob Johnson (number 54).

24. Siragusa, of the Baltimore Ravens, who dominated
    the New Jersey prep heavyweight division with a
    97–1 career record.

25. Miami.

TWO-POINT CONVERSIONS

(25 questions)

1. What jersey number does New York Giants quarterback Danny Kanell wear?
2. True or false: Fewer than 20 NFL games have ended in a tie since the league adopted its current overtime system in 1974.
3. Since Los Angeles Rams defensive back Jerry Gray won the award in the 1990 game, how many times has a defensive player been named most valuable player of the Pro Bowl (through the '98 game): none, two, or four?
4. What team did the Buffalo Bills defeat 51–3 on January 20, 1990, to advance to their first Super Bowl?
5. In the 1960s, what team's dominating defensive line was known as the "Fearsome Foursome"?
6. In what facility did the Minnesota Vikings play their home games from their inception in 1961 through '81?
7. What team did the Miami Dolphins defeat 24–21 at home in the 1985 AFC divisional playoffs: the Buffalo Bills or the Cleveland Browns?
8. Who made the "Immaculate Reception"?
9. What four-time Pro Bowl quarterback starred for the Houston Gamblers of the United States Football

League in 1984 and '85, throwing for hard-to-believe totals of 9,842 yards and 83 touchdowns?

10. What is the only team in the NFL that has never won a playoff game (through the 1997 season)?

11. True or false: No player ever has had more than three touchdown receptions in a "Monday Night Football" game.

12. What was the name of the AFL team in New York from 1960 to 1962, before it became known as the Jets: the Hudsons, the Knickerbockers, or the Titans?

13. Which Hall of Fame wide receiver holds the San Diego Chargers' all-time record for receiving yards: Lance Alworth or Charlie Joiner?

14. What team did the Los Angeles Rams defeat 20–0 at home in the 1985 NFC divisional playoffs: the Dallas Cowboys or the St. Louis Cardinals?

15. Name the Hall of Fame running back who took a handoff and scampered an NFL-record 99 yards for a touchdown against the Minnesota Vikings in 1983.

16. What jersey number does Cincinnati Bengals wide receiver Carl Pickens wear?

17. Who is the New Orleans Saints' all-time leader in receptions and receiving yards? (Hint: He played with the team from 1985 to 1993.)

18. Quarterback Dan Marino, whose NFL career began in 1983, owns the all-time league record for consecutive 3,000-yard passing seasons. Within one season either way, what's the record?

19. What jersey number does Arizona Cardinals quarterback Jake Plummer wear?

20. Quarterback Len Dawson probably wasn't quite as happy as the rest of his Kansas City Chiefs teammates after a 31–7 victory over the San Diego Chargers November 15, 1964—that was the game in which he set the all-time NFL record for fumbles in a game

by one player. Within one either way, how many fumbles did Dawson have?

21. Who is the only player in NFL history to lead the league in rushing and win the Super Bowl in the same season?

22. True or false: Troy Aikman holds the Dallas Cowboys' all-time record for passing yards in a season.

23. What was the first team to appear in a fourth Super Bowl?

24. In how many of Hall-of-Famer Don Hutson's 11 NFL seasons did he lead the league in receptions: none, eight, or ten?

25. What jersey number does Minnesota Vikings wide receiver Cris Carter wear?

ANSWERS

1. Number 13.
2. True. Through the 1997 season, there had been only 15 such games.
3. None.
4. The Los Angeles Raiders.
5. The Los Angeles Rams'. The "Foursome": Rosey Grier, Deacon Jones, Lamar Lundy, and Merlin Olsen.
6. Metropolitan Stadium in Bloomington, Minnesota.
7. The Cleveland Browns.
8. Franco Harris, the Pittsburgh Steelers running back. Late in the fourth quarter of a 1972 playoff game against the Oakland Raiders, Harris raced under a tipped pass and scooped it off his shoetops, then took it all the way in for a 60-yard touchdown in a 13–7 win.

9. Jim Kelly, who was the USFL's most valuable player in 1984.

10. The New Orleans Saints, who are 0–4 in playoff games.

11. True. The record is three, shared by six players.

12. The Titans.

13. Alworth, with 9,585 yards from 1962 to 1970. Joiner holds the club record for receptions, with 586 from 1976 to 1986.

14. The Dallas Cowboys.

15. Tony Dorsett of the Dallas Cowboys. Incredibly, the Cowboys only had 10 men on the field for that play. Fullback Ron Springs, for whom the handoff was intended, had misunderstood quarterback Danny White's play call and gone to the sideline. When White received the snap and turned around, only Dorsett was there—and the rest is history.

16. Number 81.

17. Eric Martin, with 532 catches for 7,854 yards.

18. Nine. Marino began the streak in his second season and kept it going through 1992; it ended in '93 when an injury limited him to five games played.

19. Number 16.

20. Seven.

21. Emmitt Smith of the Dallas Cowboys, who has done it three times.

22. False. Aikman's best effort—3,445 yards in 1992—ranks only third on the team's all-time list, behind Danny White's 3,980 in '83 and Roger Staubach's 3,586 in '79.

23. The Minnesota Vikings, for whom Super Bowl XI was number four.

24. Eight, with an average of 49.1 receptions in those seasons.

25. Number 80.

PLAYER
TWO

QUARTERBACK SNEAKS

(25 questions, one yard each)

1. What jersey number did quarterback Joe Montana wear throughout his NFL career?
2. With what team did former All-Pro defensive linemen Michael Carter, Fred Dean, and Tim Harris all play?
3. What NFL expansion team lost its first 26 games, in 1976 and '77?
4. Who was the NFL commissioner from 1960 to 1989?
5. By what nickname is NFL running back Craig Heyward known?
6. Name the Chicago Bears running back who scored 22 touchdowns in 1965, the highest total ever for an NFL rookie.
7. How many Super Bowls did the Cleveland Browns win?
8. How many points are awarded for a safety?
9. What team won Super Bowl XXX on January 28, 1996?
10. In what facility did the Washington Redskins play their home games before moving to a brand-new site in 1997?
11. If an official holds a clenched fist in front of his chest

and grasps his wrist with the opposite hand, what is he signaling?

12. Which of the following players was not a starting safety for the Denver Broncos in Super Bowl XXXII: Steve Atwater, Tyrone Braxton, or Dennis Smith?

13. By what nickname was Hall of Fame defensive end David Jones known? (Hint: He played for the Los Angeles Rams from 1961 to 1971, the San Diego Chargers from 1972 to 1973, and the Washington Redskins in '74.)

14. With what team did quarterback Neil O'Donnell play the first six seasons of his NFL career (1990–95) before signing as a free agent with the New York Jets in 1996?

15. What position does star defender Warren Sapp play: cornerback, linebacker, or tackle?

16. How many yards must an onside kick travel (without being touched by the receiving team) before it can be touched by the kicking team?

17. How many Super Bowls have the Philadelphia Eagles won?

18. How many yards is a team penalized for an unsportsmanlike conduct call?

19. How many yards long (goal line to end line) is an end zone?

20. How is it determined which team will receive the kickoff to start a game?

21. Who preceded Bobby Ross as coach of the Detroit Lions?

22. How many yards is an offense penalized for a false start?

23. With what team did defensive end Richard Dent play from 1983 to 1993 and for three games in '95?

24. How many two-minute warnings are there in a non-overtime NFL game?

25. How many NFL teams has Mike Ditka served as head coach?

ANSWERS

1. Number 16.
2. The San Francisco 49ers. Dean played with the team from 1981 to 1985, Carter from 1984 to 1992, and Harris from 1991 to 1992 and 1994 to 1995.
3. The Tampa Bay Buccaneers, who ended the drought by winning their final two games of the '77 season.
4. Pete Rozelle.
5. "Ironhead," a moniker he picked up at the University of Pittsburgh.
6. Gale Sayers, whose scoring plays were split between rushes (14), receptions (six), and kick returns (two).
7. None, although the Browns—who never made it to a Super Bowl—won NFL championships in 1950, '54, '55, and '64.
8. Two.
9. The Dallas Cowboys, by a 27–17 score over the Pittsburgh Steelers.
10. RFK Stadium.
11. A holding penalty.
12. Smith, whose career with the Broncos spanned 1981 to 1994 (and included three Super Bowl appearances).
13. "Deacon."
14. The Pittsburgh Steelers, with whom he started 61 games, threw for 12,867 yards and 68 touchdowns, and reached the Pro Bowl after the 1992 season.
15. Tackle.
16. Ten.

17. None, although the Eagles—who are 0–1 in the Super Bowl—won NFL championships in 1948 and '49.
18. Fifteen.
19. Ten.
20. By coin toss. The toss is called in the air by the visiting team's captain. The winner of the toss elects either to kick off or to receive, or which goal his team is to defend; if he elects to defend a certain goal, he defers the choice of kicking off or receiving to the opposing captain.
21. Wayne Fontes, who coached the Lions from the final five games of 1988 through the '96 season, going 67–71–0 and reaching the playoffs four times.
22. Five.
23. The Chicago Bears, with whom he started 146 games, had a team-record 124.5 sacks, and played in four Pro Bowls.
24. Two—one with two minutes remaining in each half.
25. Two. Ditka coached the Chicago Bears from 1982 to 1992 and has been with the New Orleans Saints since '97.

CLOUDS OF DUST

(100 questions, three yards each)

1. With what team did Hall of Fame linebacker Jack Lambert play his entire NFL career?
2. What NFL team did placekicker Kevin Butler play for from 1985 to 1995?
3. In what facility did the Buffalo Bills play their home games in 1998?
4. By what nickname was New York Jets star quarterback Joe Namath known: "Broadway Joe," "Joe Guns," or "Smokin' Joe"?
5. Who holds the NFL record for rushing yards in a single game?
6. Before being acquired by the San Francisco 49ers in a trade prior to the 1987 season, with what team did quarterback Steve Young play for parts of two NFL seasons?
7. What quarterback led the NFL in touchdown passes in 1995 and '96?
8. What do NFLers Charles Johnson, Rashaan Salaam, Kordell Stewart, and Michael Westbrook have in common?
9. With what AFC team did cornerback Albert Lewis play from 1983 to 1993, intercepting 38 passes and earning four trips to the Pro Bowl along the way?

10. According to the NFL rule book, when a ball "is dead on or behind a team's own goal line, provided the impetus came from an opponent and provided it is not a touchdown or a missed field goal," what's the call?

11. With what NFL team did Pittsburgh Steelers cornerback Donnell Woolford play from his rookie year of 1989 to '96?

12. Which one of the following NFL quarterbacks never won the Heisman Trophy: Mark Brunell, Ty Detmer, Vinny Testaverde, or Danny Wuerffel?

13. Which one of the following NFL running backs is at least six feet tall: Terrell Davis, Barry Sanders, Emmitt Smith, or Robert Smith?

14. NFL coaches Norv Turner and Dave Wannstedt worked together as assistants in the early 1990s under what coach and with what team?

15. In what facility did the Kansas City Chiefs play their home games in 1998?

16. Which quarterback went first in the 1993 NFL draft: Drew Bledsoe or Rick Mirer?

17. Of the following four "Joes," who isn't a member of the Pro Football Hall of Fame: Joe Gibbs, Joe Greene, Joe Kapp, or Joe Namath?

18. In what facility did the New England Patriots play their home games in 1998?

19. From the AFL-NFL merger in 1970 through the '97 season, which one of the following teams has a winning record in regular-season interconference play (AFC vs. NFC): the New England Patriots or the Minnesota Vikings?

20. Which one of the following teams has an all-time winning record on "Monday Night Football" (through 1997): the Cincinnati Bengals or the Oakland (and Los Angeles) Raiders?

21. Whom did Dan Reeves replace in 1997 as Atlanta Falcons coach?

22. What jersey number does Dallas Cowboys quarterback Troy Aikman wear?

23. Who is the leading rusher in Tennessee (and Houston) Oilers history?

24. What jersey number does New England Patriots quarterback Drew Bledsoe wear?

25. With what team did linebacker Cornelius Bennett play for nine seasons (1987–95) before signing as a free agent in 1996 with the Atlanta Falcons?

26. In what facility did the Seattle Seahawks play their home games in 1998?

27. What NFL team did current Detroit Lions coach Bobby Ross serve in that same capacity from 1992 to 1996?

28. What jersey number does San Francisco 49ers quarterback Steve Young wear?

29. Who is the San Francisco 49ers' career leader in passing yards and touchdown passes?

30. For what NFC team did placekicker Chip Lohmiller play from 1988 to 1994?

31. Who coached the New York Jets first: Walt Michaels or Joe Walton?

32. Which one of the following teams has an all-time winning record on ''Monday Night Football'' (through 1997): the Chicago Bears or the Seattle Seahawks?

33. Who coached the Oakland Raiders from 1969 to 1978, running up a 112–39–7 record and a Super Bowl win in the process?

34. Who is the leading rusher in Pittsburgh Steelers history?

35. How does the San Diego Chargers running back whose last name is Means spell his first name?

36. For what team did Ernest Givins catch 542 passes for 7,935 yards from 1986 to 1994?

37. In what facility did the Dallas Cowboys play their home games in 1998?

38. Name the wide receiver who caught 888 passes for 12,028 yards for the Washington Redskins from 1980 to 1993.

39. What jersey number does Indianapolis Colts running back Marshall Faulk wear?

40. What jersey number does Denver Broncos quarterback John Elway wear?

41. For what NFL team did John Stallworth amass team records of 537 receptions and 8,723 receiving yards from 1974 to 1987?

42. In what facility did the Green Bay Packers play their home games in 1998?

43. What team won Super Bowl XXVII on January 31, 1993?

44. What team won Super Bowl I on January 15, 1967?

45. Name any one of the six players whose jersey numbers have been retired by the Detroit Lions.

46. Which one of the following teams has an all-time winning record on "Monday Night Football" (through 1997): the Buffalo Bills or the Indianapolis (and Baltimore) Colts?

47. What jersey number has quarterback Warren Moon worn throughout his NFL career?

48. In what facility did the New Orleans Saints play their home games in 1998?

49. From the AFL-NFL merger in 1970 through the '97 season, which one of the following teams has a winning record in regular-season interconference play (AFC vs. NFC): the Philadelphia Eagles or the Tennessee (and Houston) Oilers?

50. With what team did quarterback Jeff Hostetler play the first nine seasons of his NFL career (1984–92)?

51. Name the NFC East running back who holds the NFL record for touchdowns in a season, with 25.

52. What team lost four of the first 11 Super Bowls: the Baltimore Colts, Dallas Cowboys, Kansas City Chiefs, or Minnesota Vikings?

53. In what city has the NFL Pro Bowl been played since 1980?

54. When a football official extends his arms over his head and presses his hands together, what is he signaling?

55. In what facility did the Philadelphia Eagles play their home games in 1998?

56. Which one of the following quarterbacks did not play at the University of Miami: Jim Kelly, Bernie Kosar, Joe Montana, or Vinny Testaverde?

57. Where did Denver Broncos quarterback John Elway play in college?

58. With what team has safety Carnell Lake played since his NFL rookie season of 1989?

59. With what team did cornerback Cris Dishman play the first nine seasons of his NFL career (1988–96) before signing as a free agent with the Washington Redskins in 1997?

60. With what team did Hall of Fame cornerback/safety Mel Renfro play his entire NFL career: the Baltimore Colts, Dallas Cowboys, Pittsburgh Steelers, or Washington Redskins?

61. With what team did Hall of Fame guard Gene Upshaw play his entire NFL career (1967–81)?

62. What position did Hall-of-Famer Merlin Olsen play: defensive tackle or tight end?

63. If an official rotates his forearms over and over again in front of his body, what is he signaling?

64. Assuming there is no penalty being enforced from a previous play, where is the ball placed on a kickoff?

65. What NFC team's colors are royal blue, gold, and white?

66. What NFC team's colors are red, pewter, black, and orange?

67. Name the Buffalo Bills running back who scored at least one touchdown in all 14 games the team played in 1975.

68. Name any two of the eight players whose jersey numbers have been retired by the Kansas City Chiefs.

69. What NFC team's colors are old gold, black, and white?

70. With what team did Hall of Fame defensive tackle Bob Lilly play his entire NFL career?

71. What NFC team's colors are Honolulu blue and silver?

72. What NFC team's colors are royal blue, metallic silver blue, and white?

73. After a missed field goal, if the ball was snapped from the 11-yard line and kicked from the 18, where does the opposing team take possession?

74. What team did the Green Bay Packers defeat 23–10 on the road in the 1997 NFC Championship Game?

75. What AFC team's colors are Columbia blue, scarlet, and white?

76. From the AFL-NFL merger in 1970 through the '97 season, which one of the following teams has a winning record in regular-season interconference play (AFC vs. NFC): the Indianapolis (and Baltimore) Colts or the Washington Redskins?

77. What AFC team's colors are navy blue, white, and gold?

78. Name any two of the seven players whose jersey numbers have been retired by the New England Patriots.

79. Which one of the following teams has an all-time

winning record on "Monday Night Football"
(through 1997): the Kansas City Chiefs or the New
York Giants?

80. What AFC team's colors are kelly green and white?
81. What AFC team's colors are blue, red, silver, and
white?
82. Name either of the two players whose jersey numbers have been retired by the Minnesota Vikings.
83. What AFC team's colors are red, gold, and white?
84. What AFC team's colors are teal, black, and gold?
85. Which NFC division put four teams (the maximum possible) into the playoffs in 1997?
86. Under the NFL postseason format that was in place as of 1998, how many wild-card teams make the playoffs in each conference?
87. What AFC team's colors are black, orange, and white?
88. What NFC team was the only NFL team to have an 11–game winning streak in the 1997 regular season?
89. Through the 1997 NFL season, the four active career leaders in games played were placekickers. Name any one of them.
90. Name all three quarterbacks who started games for the Philadelphia Eagles in 1997.
91. What jersey number did Buffalo Bills running back Thurman Thomas wear?
92. What NFC team's colors are black, blue, and silver?
93. What NFC team's colors are red, black, and white?
94. What's the name of the middle linebacker who's made a big name for himself for his shortness of stature (five-eleven) and his great play ever since he was drafted by the Miami Dolphins out of Texas Tech in 1996?
95. Name any two of the nine players whose jersey numbers have been retired by the New York Giants.
96. Which one of the following teams has an all-time

winning record on "Monday Night Football"
(through 1997): the New York Jets or the Washington Redskins?

97. From the AFL-NFL merger in 1970 through the '97
season, which one of the following teams has a winning record in regular-season interconference play
(AFC vs. NFC): the New York Giants or the St.
Louis (and Los Angeles) Rams?

98. What AFC East team did the Chicago Bears beat
36–33 in overtime on the road in their eighth game
of the 1997 season after starting the campaign 0–7?

99. What team has All-Pro cornerback Jason Sehorn
played for since being drafted in the second round
(number 59 overall) in 1994?

100. Name any one of the three players whose jersey
numbers have been retired by the St. Louis (formerly
Los Angeles) Rams.

ANSWERS

1. The Pittsburgh Steelers, with whom he played for 11
seasons (1974–84), reached nine Pro Bowls, and
twice was named NFL defensive player of the year.

2. The Chicago Bears, with whom he set team career
records for points (1,116) and field goals (243).

3. Rich Stadium in Orchard Park, New York.

4. "Broadway Joe."

5. Walter Payton, who on November 20, 1977, gained
275 yards for the Chicago Bears in a 10–7 defeat of
the Minnesota Vikings.

6. The Tampa Bay Buccaneers, with whom Young
threw for 3,217 yards, 11 touchdowns, and 21 interceptions in 19 games (all starts).

7. Brett Favre of the Green Bay Packers, with career highs of 38 in 1995 and 39 in '96.

8. They all played together at the University of Colorado.

9. The Kansas City Chiefs.

10. A touchback.

11. The Chicago Bears, with whom Woolford started all 111 games in which he played and totaled 32 interceptions.

12. Brunell. The now-Jacksonville Jaguars quarterback played at the University of Washington, where the highest honor he received was second-team All-Pac-10 (in both 1990 and '92).

13. Robert Smith of the Minnesota Vikings, who stands six-two. Davis is five-eleven, Sanders is five-eight, and Emmitt Smith is five-nine.

14. Jimmy Johnson and the Dallas Cowboys. Wannstedt was Johnson's defensive coordinator from 1989 to 1992 before being hired as head coach by the Chicago Bears; Turner was Johnson's offensive coordinator from 1991 to 1993 before taking over the Washington Redskins.

15. Arrowhead Stadium in Kansas City, Missouri.

16. Bledsoe. The New England Patriots took him with the number one pick; Mirer then went to the Seattle Seahawks with the number two pick.

17. Kapp. The former quarterback with the Minnesota Vikings (1967–69), Boston Patriots ('70), and Houston Oilers ('71) had an unspectacular career, although he is a co-holder of an NFL record for having thrown for seven touchdowns in one game (with the Vikings in '69).

18. Foxboro Stadium in Foxboro, Massachusetts.

19. The Vikings, who had a 50–48 record in games against AFC teams, compared to the Patriots' 37–57 mark against the NFC.

20. The Raiders, who were 33–16–1 on Monday nights, compared to the Bengals' 7–16.

21. June Jones, under whom the Falcons were 19–30 from 1994 to 1996.

22. Number 8.

23. Earl Campbell, who had 8,574 yards from 1978 to 1984.

24. Number 11.

25. The Buffalo Bills, with whom Bennett started all but one of the 129 games he played in, had 52.5 sacks, and played in five Pro Bowls.

26. The Kingdome in Seattle.

27. The San Diego Chargers, whom Ross led to a 47–33 record and three postseasons.

28. Number 8.

29. Joe Montana, who threw for 35,124 yards and 244 touchdowns in 14 seasons (1979–92) with the team.

30. The Washington Redskins, with whom he had 175 field goals and 787 points.

31. Michaels, who coached the team from 1977 to 1982 before giving way to Walton.

32. The Seahawks, who were 11–5 on Monday nights, compared to the Bears' 16–28.

33. John Madden.

34. Franco Harris, with 11,950 yards from 1972 to 1983.

35. Natrone.

36. The Houston Oilers.

37. Texas Stadium in Irving, Texas.

38. Art Monk.

39. Number 28.

40. Number 7.

41. The Pittsburgh Steelers.

42. Lambeau Field in Green Bay, Wisconsin.

43. The Dallas Cowboys, by a 52–17 score over the Buffalo Bills.

44. The Green Bay Packers, by a 35–10 score over the Kansas City Chiefs.
45. Dutch Clark (number 7), Bobby Layne (22), Doak Walker (37), Joe Schmidt (56), Chuck Hughes (85), Charlie Sanders (88).
46. The Colts, who were 10–8 on Monday nights, compared to the Bills' 16–19.
47. Number 1.
48. The Louisiana Superdome in New Orleans. (The Superdome is an acceptable answer.)
49. The Eagles, who had a 54–42–1 record in games against AFC teams, compared to the Oilers' 42–58–1 mark against the NFC.
50. The New York Giants, with whom he started only 25 regular-season games.
51. The Dallas Cowboys' Emmitt Smith, who accomplished the feat in 1995.
52. The Minnesota Vikings, who lost Super Bowls IV, VIII, IX, and XI.
53. Honolulu. The game was played in seven different cities in its nine years of existence prior to 1980.
54. A safety.
55. Veterans Stadium in Philadelphia.
56. Montana, who played at Notre Dame.
57. Stanford, where he was a first-team All-American as a sophomore in 1980 and a senior in '82, and from which he graduated with a degree in economics in 1983.
58. The Pittsburgh Steelers, who drafted him in the second round (number 34 overall) and immediately made him a starter.
59. The Houston Oilers, with whom he started 109 games, had 31 interceptions, and played in the Pro Bowl following the 1991 season.
60. The Cowboys, with whom he intercepted 52 passes and was elected to 10 Pro Bowls from 1964 to 1977.

61. The Oakland Raiders, with whom he played in 10 AFL or AFC championship games, three Super Bowls, and seven Pro Bowls. Upshaw currently is the executive director of the NFL Players Association.

62. Defensive tackle. Olsen, who played with the Los Angeles Rams from 1962 to 1976, was named to 14 consecutive Pro Bowls and was inducted into the Hall of Fame in 1982.

63. A false start penalty (or an illegal formation, or a kickoff or safety kick out of bounds).

64. On the kicking team's 30-yard line.

65. The St. Louis Rams.

66. The Tampa Bay Buccaneers, whose red officially is called ''Buccaneer red.''

67. O.J. Simpson, who led the league that season in total TDs (23), points (138), and rushing yards (1,817), and was named the AFC's most valuable player.

68. Jan Stenerud (number 3), Len Dawson (16), Abner Hayes (28), Stone Johnson (33), Mack Lee Hill (36), Willie Lanier (63), Bobby Bell (78), and Buck Buchanan (86).

69. The New Orleans Saints.

70. The Dallas Cowboys, with whom he played in 11 Pro Bowls and missed only one game in his 14 seasons (1961–74).

71. The Detroit Lions.

72. The Dallas Cowboys.

73. The 20-yard line. All field goals attempted and missed from inside the 20-yard line result in the defensive team taking possession on the 20.

74. The San Francisco 49ers.

75. The Tennessee Oilers.

76. The Redskins, who had a 52–43 record in games against AFC teams, compared to the Colts' 35–51–1 mark against the NFC.

77. The San Diego Chargers.
78. Steve Grogan (number 14), Gino Cappelletti (20), Mike Haynes (40), Steve Nelson (57), John Hannah (73), Jim Hunt (79), and Bob Dee (89).
79. The Chiefs, who were 16–10 on Monday nights, compared to the Giants' 14–21–1.
80. The New York Jets.
81. The New England Patriots.
82. Fran Tarkenton (number 10) and Alan Page (88).
83. The Kansas City Chiefs.
84. The Jacksonville Jaguars.
85. The Central Division. The Green Bay Packers, Tampa Bay Buccaneers, Detroit Lions, and Minnesota Vikings all qualified for the postseason; only the Chicago Bears did not.
86. Three.
87. The Cincinnati Bengals.
88. The San Francisco 49ers, who fell 13–6 at the Tampa Bay Buccaneers in week one, then didn't lose again until the Kansas City Chiefs hammered them 44–9 at K.C. nearly three months later.
89. The four: Gary Anderson (245 games played), Morten Andersen (244), Norm Johnson (243), and Eddie Murray (240).
90. Ty Detmer, Rodney Peete, and Bobby Hoying.
91. Number 34.
92. The Carolina Panthers, whose blue officially is called "Panther blue."
93. The Arizona Cardinals, whose red officially is called "Cardinal red."
94. Zach Thomas.
95. Ray Flaherty (number 1), Mel Hein (7), Phil Simms (11), Y.A. Tittle (14), Al Blozis (32), Joe Morrison (40), Charlie Conerly (42), Ken Strong (50), and Lawrence Taylor (56).

96. The Redskins, who were 23–21 on Monday nights, compared to the Jets' 9–16.
97. The Rams, who had a 51–50 record in games against AFC teams, compared to the Giants' dead-even 44–44 mark against the AFC.
98. The Miami Dolphins.
99. The New York Giants.
100. Bob Waterfield (number 7), Merlin Olsen (74), and Jackie Slater (78).

QUICK OUTS

(75 questions, five yards each)

1. Who preceded Vince Tobin as head coach of the Arizona Cardinals?
2. True or false: O.A. "Bum" Phillips' six seasons as coach of the Houston Oilers (1975–80) represents the longest tenure of any coach in Oilers history.
3. Denver Broncos coach Mike Shanahan's only previous head coaching experience came in 1988 and '89 with what NFL team?
4. What's the most yardage longtime Giants running back Rodney Hampton ever rushed for in an NFL season: 1,182, 1,382, or 1,582?
5. With which team did cornerback Troy Vincent play the first four seasons of his NFL career (1992–95) before signing as a free agent with the Philadelphia Eagles: the Detroit Lions, Miami Dolphins, or Washington Redskins?
6. Where did Kansas City Chiefs linebacker Derrick Thomas play in college?
7. Name the player who led the NFL in rushing in 1983, '84, '86, and '88.
8. True or false: Walter Payton caught more passes than any other player in Chicago Bears history.
9. True or false: Although Minnesota chose Randy

Moss of Marshall in the first round of the 1998 draft, neither of the Vikings' star wide receivers of the past several seasons—Cris Carter and Jake Reed—is a former first-round pick.

10. In what facility did the Atlanta Falcons play their home games in 1998?

11. Who is the New York Giants' all-time leader in passing yards?

12. Before what season did the Rams move to St. Louis from Los Angeles?

13. True or false: John Robinson, who coached the Los Angeles Rams from 1983 to 1991, had a losing record with the team.

14. What jersey number does Jacksonville Jaguars quarterback Mark Brunell wear?

15. True or false: Quarterback Jeff Hostetler never has played in the Pro Bowl.

16. With what team did Hall of Fame end Raymond Berry play his entire NFL career (1955–67)?

17. In what stadium did the Green Bay Packers defeat the New England Patriots in Super Bowl XXXI?

18. There have been five players in NFL (and AFL) history with the last name Bingham. Name any one of them.

19. What jersey number does Pittsburgh Steelers quarterback Kordell Stewart wear?

20. True or false: Cornerback Deion Sanders never has reached double figures in interceptions in a season.

21. How does the St. Louis Rams defensive tackle whose last name is Farr spell his first name?

22. In what facility did the New York Jets play their home games in 1998?

23. True or false: Quarterback Steve Bono has played for both the Minnesota Vikings and Pittsburgh Steelers.

24. What jersey number does Green Bay Packers defensive end Reggie White wear?

25. What jersey number does Dallas Cowboys wide receiver Michael Irvin wear?

26. True or false: No team has ever had as many as five safeties in a single NFL season.

27. For how many seasons was Barry Switzer coach of the Dallas Cowboys?

28. What NFL team has the Mara family owned since 1925?

29. With what NFL team was current Green Bay Packers coach Mike Holmgren an assistant from 1986 to 1991?

30. Name any two of the three NFL teams running back Craig Heyward played with before signing as a free agent with the St. Louis Rams in 1997.

31. Where did former Heisman Trophy winner Desmond Howard, who's been in the NFL since 1992, play in college?

32. In what facility did the Indianapolis Colts play their home games in 1998?

33. Don Bosseler had a solid career as a fullback from 1957 to 1964 with what team: the Pittsburgh Steelers or the Washington Redskins?

34. True or false: Bill Parcells had a losing record (including playoffs) as coach of the New England Patriots (1993–96).

35. Who is the New York Jets' career rushing leader? (Hint: He played for the team from 1981 to 1992.)

36. Who is the Oakland Raiders' career passing leader in both yards and touchdowns?

37. Jerry Hill had a solid career as a running back from 1961 to 1970 with what team: the Baltimore Colts or the Philadelphia Eagles?

38. In what facility did the Miami Dolphins play their home games in 1998?

39. True or false: New York Giants coach Jim Fassel previously served the team as an assistant coach.
40. True or false: Denver Broncos quarterback John Elway never has thrown as many as 20 interceptions in a season.
41. True or false: No player in Chicago Bears history ever has had as many as 100 receptions in a season.
42. Who coached the San Diego Chargers from 1978 to 1986, compiling a 72–60 record and leading the team to three AFC West titles and four postseason appearances?
43. True or false: Hall of Fame wide receiver Charley Taylor played running back as a Washington Redskins rookie in 1964.
44. James Hunter had a solid career as a defensive back from 1976 to 1982 with what team: the Detroit Lions or the New Orleans Saints?
45. What team won Super Bowl XXV on January 27, 1991?
46. Which one of the following superstar quarterbacks never has completed at least 65 percent of his pass attempts in an NFL season: the Dallas Cowboys' Troy Aikman, the Miami Dolphins' Dan Marino, or the San Francisco 49ers' Steve Young?
47. What quarterback starred for the St. Louis Cardinals from 1966 to 1983 before finishing his career in '84 with the Washington Redskins?
48. True or false: Vince Lombardi amassed more career victories than any other coach in Green Bay Packers history.
49. In what facility did the San Diego Chargers play their home games in 1998?
50. True or false: No team has ever been shut out in the Super Bowl.
51. True or false: Defensive end Reggie White has averaged more than a sack a game in his NFL career.

52. Which one of the following former or current NFL placekickers is "left-footed": Morten Anderson, Nick Lowery, Mark Moseley, or Pete Stoyanovich?

53. True or false: The Miami Dolphins' 14–2 record in 1984 was only the second-best mark in the NFL that year.

54. True or false: Quarterback Bernie Kosar once played for the Atlanta Falcons.

55. What is longtime NFL linebacker Pepper Johnson's actual first name: Frederick, Marcus, or Thomas?

56. Which NFL team drafted current Jacksonville Jaguars quarterback Mark Brunell back in 1993: the Atlanta Falcons, the Green Bay Packers, or the Jaguars?

57. In what facility did the San Francisco 49ers play their home games in 1998?

58. What was the nickname of Alphonse Emil Leemans, who starred as a quarterback, fullback, and defensive back for the New York Giants from 1936 to 1943: "Duke," "Dutch," or "Tuffy"?

59. True or false: No NFL player ever has kicked three field goals of 50 yards or more in a single game.

60. Name either of the NFL teams linebacker Bill Romanowski played with before signing as a free agent with the Denver Broncos in 1996.

61. With what team did safety Eugene Robinson play the first 11 seasons of his NFL career (1985–95) before being traded to the Green Bay Packers in 1996?

62. Which one of the following teams *hasn't* wide receiver/kick returner Eric Metcalf played for: the Atlanta Falcons, Cleveland Browns, Minnesota Vikings, or San Diego Chargers?

63. True or false: Hall of Fame running back Larry Csonka once played for the New York Giants.

64. In what facility did the Cincinnati Bengals play their home games in 1998?

65. True or false: Hall of Fame quarterback Roger Stau-

bach played his entire NFL career with the Dallas
Cowboys.

66. Which of the following teams was in the NFL—not
the AFL—in 1969, the last season before the
leagues' merger: the Baltimore Colts, Cincinnati
Bengals, Denver Broncos, or San Diego Chargers?

67. Which of the following teams was in the AFL—not
the NFL—in 1969, the last season before the
leagues' merger: the Cleveland Browns, Miami Dolphins, Pittsburgh Steelers, or Washington Redskins?

68. True or false: Quarterback Drew Bledsoe entered the
NFL draft after his sophomore season in college.

69. True or false: Tennessee Oilers defensive end Ken-
drick Burton and Miami Dolphins defensive tackle
Shane Burton are brothers.

70. Frank Minnifield had a solid career as a defensive
back from 1984 to 1992 with what team: the Buffalo
Bills or the Cleveland Browns?

71. True or false: The Green Bay Packers have an all-
time winning regular-season record against the Chicago Bears.

72. True or false: The Miami Dolphins have an all-time
winning regular-season record against the New York
Jets.

73. Through 1997, how many times had Green Bay
Packers quarterback Brett Favre posted a passer rating of at least 100.0 in an NFL season: none, once,
or twice?

74. In what facility did the Tampa Bay Buccaneers play
their home games in 1998?

75. What NFL team did safety Marty Carter, cornerback
Tom Carter, and fullback Tony Carter play for in
1997?

ANSWERS

1. Buddy Ryan, under whom the Cardinals went 12–20 in 1994 and '95.

2. True. Phillips had a 59–38 mark with the team; his 59 wins is 15 more than Jack Pardee's second-highest Oilers win total.

3. The Los Angeles Raiders, who were 7–9 under Shanahan in 1988 and 1–3 in '89 before Shanahan was fired.

4. Hampton rushed for 1,182 yards, in 1995. Five times ('91–95) Hampton rushed for at least 1,000 yards, but in the Giants' grind-it-out offense, he never reached even 1,200 yards.

5. The Dolphins, for whom he started 55 games and had 14 interceptions.

6. Alabama, where Thomas won the Butkus Award as the nation's best linebacker in 1988 before being drafted by the Chiefs with the number four overall pick in the '89 draft.

7. Eric Dickerson, who did it in 1983 (1,808 yards), '84 (2,105), and '86 (1,821) as a member of the Los Angeles Rams, and in '88 (1,659) with the Indianapolis Colts.

8. True. Payton's 492 receptions from 1975 to 1987 eclipsed Johnny Morris's old team record by 136. Morris still holds the team record for receiving yards, however, with 5,059; Payton stands third at 4,538.

9. True. Carter, who played his first three seasons (1987–89) with the Philadelphia Eagles, was a fourth-rounder in the '87 supplemental draft; Reed was taken by the Vikings in the third round in 1991.

10. The Georgia Dome in Atlanta.

11. Phil Simms, who threw for 33,462 yards from 1979 to 1993.

12. The 1995 season.

13. False. Under Robinson the Rams were 79–74 and reached the playoffs six times.

14. Number 8.

15. False. Hostetler played in the Pro Bowl after the 1994 season, when he threw for 3,334 yards and 20 touchdowns as a member of the Los Angeles Raiders.

16. The Baltimore Colts, with whom he had 631 receptions for 9,275 yards and 68 touchdowns.

17. The Louisiana Superdome in New Orleans, before 72,301 fans.

18. Craig Bingham (linebacker, Pittsburgh Steelers 1982–84, '87, San Diego Chargers '85); Don Bingham (halfback, Chicago Bears '56); Dwight Bingham (defensive end, Atlanta Falcons '87); Gregg Bingham (linebacker, Houston Oilers 1973–84); Guy Bingham (center/guard/tackle, New York Jets 1980–88, Atlanta 1989–91, Washington Redskins 1992–93).

19. Number 10.

20. True. Sanders had a career-high and NFC-leading seven pickoffs in 1993 when he was with the Atlanta Falcons.

21. D'Marco.

22. The Meadowlands in East Rutherford, New Jersey. (Giants Stadium is an acceptable answer.)

23. True. Bono was a Vikings backup his first two seasons in the NFL (1985 and '86) and filled the same role for the Steelers the next two seasons.

24. Number 92.

25. Number 88.

26. True. The record is four, shared by four teams: the 1927 Cleveland Browns, '62 Detroit Lions, '93 Se-

attle Seahawks, and '96 San Francisco 49ers.

27 Four, from 1994 to 1997, during which time the Cowboys were 40–24 in the regular season, had three playoff appearances, and won one Super Bowl.

28. The New York Giants. Tim Mara, who brought the Giants to the league in 1925, and his son Wellington, who first joined the operation in 1937, both were enshrined in the Pro Football Hall of Fame.

29. The San Francisco 49ers, as quarterbacks coach from 1986 to 1988 and offensive coordinator from 1989 to 1991.

30. The New Orleans Saints (1988–92), Chicago Bears ('93), and Atlanta Falcons (1994–96).

31. Michigan, where Howard won the Heisman as a senior in 1991 before completing his degree in communication studies.

32. The RCA Dome in Indianapolis.

33. The Redskins, with whom Bosseler amassed career marks of 775 rushes for 3,112 yards, 136 receptions for 1,083 yards, and 23 touchdowns.

34. False. Parcells' record was dead-even at 34–34.

35. Freeman McNeil, with 8,074 yards.

36. Ken Stabler, who threw for 19,078 yards and 150 touchdowns with the team from 1970 to 1979.

37. The Colts, with whom Hill amassed career marks of 706 rushes for 2,668 yards, 117 receptions for 970 yards, and 25 touchdowns.

38. Pro Player Stadium in Miami.

39. True. Fassel was the Giants' quarterbacks coach in 1991 and offensive coordinator in '92.

40. False. Elway did it once, in 1985, his third year in the NFL, when he threw an AFC-worst 23. (In Elway's defense, he attempted an NFL-high 605 passes that season.)

41. True. Johnny Morris's 93 catches in 1964 still stands as the team high.

42. Don Coryell.
43. True. Taylor, who played with the Redskins from 1964 to 1975 and in '77, was the team's leading rusher with 755 yards in '64, when he was named NFL rookie of the year. He made the switch to fulltime wide receiver during the '66 season.
44. The Lions, with whom Hunter amassed career marks of 27 interceptions for 279 yards, with one touchdown.
45. The New York Giants, by a 20–19 score over the Buffalo Bills.
46. Marino, whose best effort was 64.2 percent way back in 1984. Through the 1997 season, Aikman had done it twice, in 1991 (65.3) and '93 (69.1); Young had done it a whopping seven times, in '89 (69.6), '92 (66.7), '93 (68.0), '94 (70.3), '95 (66.9), '96 (67.7), and '97 (67.7).
47. Jim Hart, who threw for 34,665 yards, 209 touchdowns, and 247 interceptions in his 19-year NFL career.
48. False. Earl "Curly" Lambeau, who coached the Packers from 1921 through '49, had a record of 212–106–21; Lombardi, who coached the team from 1957 through '67, was 98–30–4.
49. Qualcomm Stadium in San Diego.
50. True. The Miami Dolphins, who were beaten 24–3 by the Dallas Cowboys in Super Bowl VI, hold the record for fewest points scored.
51. False. The NFL's leader in sacks (since the league began keeping the statistic in 1982) has only had at least as many sacks as games played three times in his career, and not once since 1988.
52. Anderson, a regular Pro Bowler who played for the New Orleans Saints from 1982 to 1994 before signing as a free agent with the Atlanta Falcons in '95.
53. True. The 15–1 San Francisco 49ers—who would go

on to defeat the Dolphins 38–16 in Super Bowl XIX—had the best record.

54. False. Kosar, who retired prior to the 1997 season, played for the Cleveland Browns from 1985 to 1993, the Dallas Cowboys for the last half of '93, and the Miami Dolphins from 1994 to 1996.

55. Thomas. The nickname "Pepper" came from an aunt who watched two-year-old Thomas sprinkle pepper on his cereal, take a big bite, and then sprinkle on some more.

56. The Packers, who took him in the fifth round (number 118 overall) and eventually traded him to the Jaguars in 1995.

57. 3Com Park in San Francisco.

58. "Tuffy." Leemans concluded his career with totals of 2,318 passing yards and 25 passing touchdowns, 3,132 rushing yards and 17 rushing TDs, 422 receiving yards and three receiving TDs, and four interceptions.

59. False. It's been done by one player, Morten Andersen of the Atlanta Falcons, in a 19–14 defeat of the New Orleans Saints in 1995.

60. The San Francisco 49ers (1988–93), with whom he started 76 of the 96 games he played in, and the Philadelphia Eagles (1994–95), with whom he started 31 of 32 games.

61. The Seattle Seahawks, with whom Robinson had 42 interceptions and two Pro Bowl seasons (1992 and '93) before being traded for linebacker Matt La-Bounty.

62. The Vikings. Metcalf was with the Browns from 1989 to 1994 and the Falcons in '95 and '96 before signing with the Chargers prior to the '97 season.

63. True. Csonka, best-known for his exploits as a member of the Miami Dolphins, played for the Giants from 1976 to 1978, compiling 1,344 of his 8,081

career rushing yards and 11 of his 68 career touchdowns.

64. Cinergy Field in Cincinnati.

65. True. Staubach played for the Cowboys from 1969 to 1979, leading them to four NFC titles and a pair of Super Bowl wins.

66. The Colts, who have been in the NFL since their inception in 1953.

67. The Dolphins, who were in the AFL from their inception in 1966 until the merger.

68. False—but he did leave school early. Bledsoe played through his junior season at Washington State before entering the 1993 draft.

69. False. They are unrelated.

70. The Browns, with whom Minnifield amassed career marks of 20 interceptions for 124 yards.

71. False. Through the 1997 season, Chicago held an 81–67–6 advantage—but the Packers had won eight straight in the series and 10 out of 11.

72. True. Through the 1997 season, Miami held a 33–30–1 advantage.

73. None. Favre achieved his best rating, 99.5, in 1995.

74. Houlihan's Stadium in Tampa. ("Houlihan" Stadium is not an acceptable answer.)

75. The Chicago Bears.

TIGHT END CURLS

(50 questions, seven yards each)

1. Name the three teams Hall of Fame tight end Mike Ditka played for in his 12-year career.

2. With what team did star linebacker Dave Robinson play for the first 10 years (1963–72) of his 12-year NFL career: the Detroit Lions, Green Bay Packers, or New York Giants?

3. Name the wide receiver who caught 478 passes for 7,636 yards and 52 touchdowns with the Minnesota Vikings from 1985 to 1993.

4. Where did wide receiver Carl Pickens play in college: Arizona State, Louisiana State, Tennessee, or Wyoming?

5. How many head coaches did the Dallas Cowboys have before Barry Switzer, who took the job in 1994?

6. In how many seasons has Miami Dolphins quarterback Dan Marino led the NFL in completions? (Hint: The all-time record is five.)

7. Name the former St. Louis Cardinals star who racked up 7,999 yards rushing with the team from 1979 to 1986.

8. Jacksonville coach Tom Coughlin coached for three

seasons in college at what school before taking over the Jaguars in 1995?

9. With what team did star tight end Charlie Sanders play for his entire 10-year NFL career (1968–77): the Baltimore Colts, Detroit Lions, or New York Giants?

10. Atlanta Falcons coach Dan Reeves spent his entire eight-year NFL playing career (1965–72) with what team?

11. Which Philadelphia Eagles player led the NFC in 1995 with 13 sacks: William Fuller, Mike Mamula, or William Thomas?

12. Where did Buffalo Bills defensive end Bruce Smith play in college?

13. What player led the AFC in rushing in 1990, '91, and '93?

14. What team won Super Bowl XXI on January 25, 1987?

15. Name the Arizona running back who in 1996 set the all-time Cardinals record for rushing yards in a single game, with 214.

16. Who was the Dallas Cowboys' placekicker from 1978 to 1986?

17. What jersey number does Denver Broncos running back Terrell Davis wear?

18. Who is the Philadelphia Eagles' all-time passing leader?

19. Who is the St. Louis Rams' all-time leader in receptions and receiving yards? (Hint: He played with the team when it was in Los Angeles.)

20. How many NFL teams had a better regular-season record in 1992 than the Dallas Cowboys, who went on to win the Super Bowl?

21. What Kansas City Chiefs player led the AFC in 1993 with 15 sacks?

22. With what team did Hall of Fame defensive tackle Buck Buchanan play his entire pro career (1963–75)?

23. What was Hall of Fame running back Earl Campbell's listed playing weight: 193, 213, 233, or 253?

24. How many Super Bowls have the Washington Redskins played in?

25. Who coached the Tampa Bay Buccaneers from their inception in 1976 through '84?

26. What position did three-time Pro Bowler Drew Pearson, who starred for the Dallas Cowboys from 1973 to 1983, play?

27. What jersey number does Kansas City Chiefs linebacker Derrick Thomas wear?

28. Three players share the record for points scored in a single Super Bowl game, with 18; all three did it as members of the San Francisco 49ers. Name any two of them.

29. When an official extends one arm in front of his body and points it toward the defensive team's goal, what is he signaling?

30. Name the NFL player whose hometown of Swann Station, North Carolina, is named for his ancestors.

31. With what team did linebacker Bryce Paup play the first five seasons of his NFL career (1990–94) before signing as a free agent with the Buffalo Bills in 1995?

32. Where did quarterback Warren Moon play in college?

33. Whom did Bruce Coslet replace seven games into the 1996 season as coach of the Cincinnati Bengals?

34. What NFL team was coached by John Mackovic from 1983 to 1986?

35. Name both NFL teams with which linebacker Seth Joyner played before signing with the Green Bay Packers in 1997.

36. Who was the first African-American to play quarterback in the NFL? (Hint: He was very aptly named.)

37. Who was the AFC's top-rated passer in 1990 and

'91: John Elway, Boomer Esiason, Jim Kelly, or Dan Marino?

38. What NFC Central wide receiver led the NFL in receptions in 1989, '92, and '93?

39. What "speedy" NFC East wide receiver led his conference in receiving yards in 1983 and '85?

40. What Los Angeles Raiders safety led the NFL in 1991 with eight interceptions? (Hint: He is a certain future Hall-of-Famer.)

41. For what team did Audray McMillan play when he led the NFC (and tied for the NFL lead) in 1992 with eight interceptions?

42. Name the brother of Hall of Fame running back Walter Payton who also played in the NFL.

43. Name the tight end who led the AFC in 1994 with 96 receptions.

44. What is the nickname of Chicago Bears offensive tackle James Williams?

45. What New Orleans Saints running back led the NFL in 1981 with 1,674 rushing yards?

46. Has there ever been an NFL player who was shorter than five feet?

47. What position did nine-time Pro Bowler Maxie Baughan, who starred for the Philadelphia Eagles (1960–65) and Los Angeles Rams (1966–70), play?

48. For what NFL team did running back Herschel Walker play from 1992 to 1994?

49. Name either of the colleges where Dennis Green was a head coach.

50. Which of the following NFLers did not play at Ohio State: Cris Carter, Eddie George, Raymont Harris, or Darren Woodson?

ANSWERS

1. The Chicago Bears (1961–66), Philadelphia Eagles (1967–68), and Dallas Cowboys (1969–72).
2. The Packers, with whom the six-foot-three-inch, 245-pound Robinson teamed for several years with Ray Nitschke and Leroy Caffey to comprise one of the game's best-ever linebacker corps. Robinson finished his career in '73 and '74 with the Washington Redskins.
3. Anthony Carter, whose team records for receiving yards and touchdown catches were broken by Cris Carter in 1997.
4. Tennessee, where he gained first-team All-America honors as a junior in 1991 before skipping his senior season to enter the '92 NFL draft.
5. Two: Tom Landry, who coached the team from its inception in 1960 through 1988; and Jimmy Johnson, who had the job from 1989 to 1993.
6. Five: in 1984, '85, '86, '88, and '92. Marino co-owns the record with Hall-of-Famer Sammy Baugh, who did it in 1937, '43, '45, '47, and '48.
7. Ottis "O.J." Anderson, who then played until 1992 with the New York Giants and finished his career with 10,273 yards rushing.
8. Boston College, where the Eagles were 20–12–1 under Coughlin from 1991 to 1993.
9. The Lions, with whom the six-foot-four-inch, 235-pound Sanders played in seven Pro Bowls and led his team in receptions four times.
10. The Dallas Cowboys, for whom Reeves played halfback, rushing for 1,990 yards and 25 touchdowns and catching 129 passes for 1,693 yards and 17 more TDs.

11. Fuller, who recorded 13 more sacks for the Eagles in 1996 but whose best NFL season came in '91, when he had an AFC-leading 15 sacks for the Houston Oilers. Mamula had 5.5 sacks in '95, his rookie season; Thomas had only 2.0.

12. Virginia Tech, where Smith won the Outland Trophy as the nation's best lineman as a senior in 1984 before being selected by the Bills as the number one overall pick in the '85 draft.

13. Thurman Thomas of the Buffalo Bills, with 1,297 in 1990, 1,407 in '91, and 1,315 in '93.

14. The New York Giants, by a 39–20 score over the Denver Broncos.

15. LeShon Johnson, who did it in a 28–14 win at the New Orleans Saints. The highlights: On consecutive fourth-quarter possessions, Johnson had touchdown runs of 56 and 70 yards.

16. Rafael Septien, who holds the team records for field goals (162) and points scored (874).

17. Number 30.

18. Ron Jaworski, who threw for 26,963 yards from 1977 to 1986.

19. Henry Ellard, who caught 593 passes for 9,761 yards with the team from 1983 to 1993.

20. One: the San Francisco 49ers, who were 14–2 to Dallas' 13–3.

21. Neil Smith, a defensive end.

22. The Kansas City Chiefs, with whom he missed only one game in 13 seasons.

23. The five-foot-eleven-inch Campbell was listed at 233 pounds.

24. Five. They have a 3–2 record in those games.

25. John McKay, under whom the Bucs were 45–91–1.

26. Wide receiver.

27. Number 58.

28. The players: running back Roger Craig, in Super

Bowl XIX; wide receiver Jerry Rice, in Super Bowl XXIX; and running back Ricky Watters, also in Super Bowl XXIX.

29. A first down for the offense.

30. Eric Swann, the in-his-prime defensive tackle of the Arizona Cardinals.

31. The Green Bay Packers, with whom he had 32.5 sacks and four interceptions in 64 games and reached the Pro Bowl after the 1994 season.

32. The University of Washington, where he was named Pac-8 player of the year and led the Huskies to a 27–20 upset of Michigan in the Rose Bowl as a senior in 1977.

33. Dave Shula, who started as coach in 1992 and amassed a 19–52 record before being fired.

34. The Kansas City Chiefs, who were 30–35 with one postseason appearance (in 1986) under Mackovic.

35. The Philadelphia Eagles, with whom he started 113 games from 1986 to 1993, and Arizona Cardinals, with whom he started 48 games from 1994 to 1996.

36. Willie Thrower of the Chicago Bears, who made his debut October 18, 1953, in a loss to the San Francisco 49ers. Unfortunately, it was the only appearance Thrower would make in the league. His "career" numbers: three completions in eight attempts, 27 yards, one interception.

37. Kelly of the Buffalo Bills, with a 101.2 rating in 1990 and a 97.6 rating in '91.

38. Sterling Sharpe of the Green Bay Packers, with 90 in 1989, 108 in '92, and 112 in '93.

39. Mike Quick of the Philadelphia Eagles, with 1,409 in 1983 and 1,247 in '85.

40. Ronnie Lott, who also led the NFL in pickoffs in 1986, when he had 10 for the San Francisco 49ers.

41. The Minnesota Vikings, for whom he played from 1989 to 1993.

42. Eddie Payton, whose journeyman NFL career (spent mostly as a return specialist) included stints with the Cleveland Browns and Detroit Lions (both in '77), Kansas City Chiefs ('78), and Minnesota Vikings (1980–82).

43. Ben Coates of the New England Patriots.

44. "Big Cat"—a fitting name for a six-foot-seven-inch, 340-pounder.

45. George Rogers, who was a rookie that year after being drafted number one overall out of the University of South Carolina.

46. No. The shortest player ever was five-foot-one-inch Jack "Soapy" Shapiro, a running back who played in one game with the Staten Island Stapletons in 1929.

47. Linebacker.

48. The Philadelphia Eagles, for whom he rushed for 2,344 yards and 14 touchdowns, caught 163 passes for 1,388 yards and seven TDs, and returned one kickoff for a score.

49. Northwestern, where he was 10–45 from 1981 to 1985, and Stanford, where he was 16–17 from 1989 to 1991.

50. Woodson, a Dallas Cowboys Pro Bowl safety who starred at Arizona State.

GAPING HOLES

(50 questions, 10 yards each)

1. Where did safety LeRoy Butler, a three-time Pro Bowler with the Green Bay Packers through the 1997 season, play in college?

2. With what team did Hall of Fame linebacker Joe Schmidt play his entire 13-year NFL career?

3. What team did running back Larry Brown, who led the NFL in rushing in 1970 with 1,125 yards, play for?

4. What player did the Indianapolis Colts select with the number one overall pick in the 1990 NFL draft?

5. Which coach holds the all-time NFL record for post-season losses, with 17: Bud Grant, Tom Landry, or Don Shula?

6. Who coached the Phoenix Cardinals from 1990 to 1993?

7. What city has hosted the most Super Bowls: Miami, New Orleans, or Pasadena, California.?

8. With what team did Hall of Fame center/linebacker Chuck Bednarik play his entire NFL career (1949–62)?

9. For how many seasons did Dan Reeves coach the New York Giants before being fired after the 1996 campaign?

143

10. Name the Chicago Bears fullback who scored on an 11-yard run in the team's 46–10 defeat of the New England Patriots in Super Bowl XX.

11. With what team did kicker John Kasay play his first four NFL seasons (1991–94) before signing as a free agent with the Carolina Panthers in 1995?

12. With what team did linebacker Hardy Nickerson play his first six NFL seasons (1987–92) before signing as a free agent with the Tampa Bay Buccaneers in 1993?

13. What NFL team did current Philadelphia Eagles coach Ray Rhodes serve as defensive coordinator in 1992 and '93?

14. Everybody knows Miami Dolphins head coach Jimmy Johnson succeeded Don Shula in that position, but whom did Shula succeed?

15. In what city did the Redskins play before moving to Washington, D.C., in 1937: Baltimore, Boston, or Buffalo?

16. What is Green Bay Packers quarterback Brett Favre's middle name: Laurent, Loren, or Lorenzo?

17. Name any two of the eight men who coached the Detroit Lions in the 1930s and '40s.

18. The 1984 Miami Dolphins hold the NFL record for most net yards (rushing and passing) gained in a season, with how many: 4,936, 5,936, 6,936, or 7,936?

19. With what team did defensive end Gabe Wilkins play his first four NFL seasons (1994–97) before signing as a free agent with the San Francisco 49ers in 1998?

20. With what team did defensive tackle Santana Dotson play his first four NFL seasons (1992–95) before signing as a free agent with the Green Bay Packers in 1996?

21. Five NFL teams have had 1–15 seasons, all since 1980. Name any three of them.

22. Name the participatory journalist who wrote the

book *Paper Lion* after spending the 1965 preseason with the Detroit Lions as a 36-year-old "rookie" quarterback.

23. Which of the following running backs was not selected to play in the 1997 Pro Bowl: the Washington Redskins' Terry Allen, the Detroit Lions' Barry Sanders, the Dallas Cowboys' Emmitt Smith, or the Philadelphia Eagles' Ricky Watters?

24. What former Detroit Lions player rushed for 1,303 yards and 13 touchdowns as a rookie in 1980?

25. Who kicked the longest field goal in NFL history, a 63-yarder in 1970?

26. The Pro Football Hall of Fame Class of 1997 consists of four men: one affiliated with the New York Giants; one with the Baltimore Colts and Miami Dolphins; one with the Pittsburgh Steelers and Kansas City Chiefs; and one with the New England Patriots and Los Angeles Raiders. Name any of the four.

27. Wide receiver Ernie Mills was a member of the Carolina Panthers in 1997, then signed as a free agent with the Dallas Cowboys in '98. With what AFC team did he play his first six pro seasons (1991–96)?

28. The Pro Football Hall of Fame Class of 1996 consists of five men: one affiliated with the Washington Redskins; one with the St. Louis Cardinals; one with the Dallas Cowboys; one with the Detroit Lions; and one with the Houston Oilers, Cincinnati Bengals, and San Diego Chargers. Name any of the five.

29. What offensive tackle did the Atlanta Falcons draft in the first round (number eight overall) in 1992 with the pick they'd received earlier that year from the Green Bay Packers for the rights to quarterback Brett Favre?

30. What current NFL star in 1991 became the first non-college player drafted by a league team since Emil

"Six Yard" Sitko by the Los Angeles Rams in 1946?

31. With what team did former defensive lineman Fred Smerlas play the first 11 seasons of his 14-year NFL career (1979–89)?

32. What current NFL running back won the Heisman Trophy in 1994?

33. Where did running back Adrian Murrell, traded in 1998 by the New York Jets to the Arizona Cardinals, play in college: Western Illinois, Western Kentucky, Western Michigan, or West Virginia?

34. Name both NFL teams wide receiver Anthony Miller played with before signing as a free agent with the Dallas Cowboys in 1997.

35. Name the placekicker who holds the Cincinnati Bengals' career scoring record, with 1,151 points. (Hint: He played with the team from 1980 to 1992.)

36. What NFL team was coached by Bud Carson for all of 1989 and the first nine games of '90, and by Jim Shofner for the final seven games of '90?

37. What NFL team was coached by John Ralston from 1972 to 1976?

38. Who is the leading rusher in Indianapolis Colts history? (Hint: He played for the franchise when it was in Baltimore.)

39. Jerry Rice's San Francisco 49ers career began in 1985; his first season leading the team in receptions was '86, when he had, fittingly, 86. But Rice was only the team's second-leading receiver in '87 and '88. Name the player who finished first both years. (Hint: He wasn't a wide receiver.)

40. What six-foot-two-inch, 240-pound running back set a Kansas City Chiefs single-game rushing record with 200 yards in a 1990 game?

41. Who is the leading rusher in Miami Dolphins history?

42. In how many of the Pittsburgh Steelers' four Super Bowl wins was Hall of Fame quarterback Terry Bradshaw named most valuable player?

43. With what team did Hall of Fame tackle Roosevelt Brown play his entire NFL career (1953–65)?

44. What team won Super Bowl VII on January 14, 1973?

45. With what NFC team did four-time Pro Bowl safety Nolan Cromwell play his entire 11-year NFL career (1977–87)?

46. What is Dallas Cowboys cornerback Deion Sanders's middle name: Elwynn, Luwynn, or Wynn?

47. Name any one of the three men who coached the Los Angeles Rams in the 1950s.

48. With what team did Hall of Fame linebacker Bobby Bell play his entire AFL and NFL career (1963–74)?

49. For how many seasons did Hall of Fame coach Chuck Noll lead the Pittsburgh Steelers: 14, 17, 20, or 23?

50. Which player led the Detroit Lions in rushing in three of the four seasons before Barry Sanders' arrival in 1989: Dexter Bussey, Garry James, or James Jones?

ANSWERS

1. Florida State, from 1986 to 1989.
2. The Detroit Lions (1953–65). Schmidt had 24 interceptions in his career and was a team captain for nine years.
3. The Washington Redskins, for whom he rushed for 5,875 yards from 1969 to 1976.
4. Jeff George, a University of Illinois quarterback.

5. Shula, who lost a combined 17 playoff games with the Baltimore Colts and Miami Dolphins. Landry finished his career with 16 playoff losses; Grant finished with 12.

6. Joe Bugel, under whom the Cardinals were 20–44 and had their best season in 1993, when they were 7–9.

7. New Orleans, with eight. Miami has hosted seven Super Bowls, Pasadena five.

8. The Philadelphia Eagles, with whom he made eight Pro Bowls.

9. Four. From 1993 to 1996 Reeves led the Giants to a 31–33 record and one playoff victory.

10. Matt Suhey, who played with the team from 1980 to 1989.

11. The Seattle Seahawks, with whom he converted 82 of 105 field-goal attempts and scored 341 points.

12. The Pittsburgh Steelers, with whom he started 61 games.

13. The Green Bay Packers.

14. George Wilson, the only other head coach in team history. Wilson led the expansion Dolphins to a 15–39–2 mark from 1966 to 1969.

15. Boston, where they played from 1932 to 1936. (They were called the Boston Braves in '32 before changing their name to Redskins the next season.)

16. Lorenzo.

17. Hal "Tubby" Griffen (1930), George "Potsy" Clark (1931–36, '40), Earl "Dutch" Clark (1937–38), Elmer "Gus" Henderson ('39), Bill Edwards (1941–42), John Karcis ('42), Charles "Gus" Dorais (1943–47), and Alvin "Bo" McMillin (1948–49).

18. The Dolphins had 6,936 net yards.

19. The Green Bay Packers, with whom he started 25 games—including all 16 in the team's NFC cham-

pionship season of 1997—and compiled 12.5 sacks, one interception, and two touchdowns.

20. The Tampa Bay Buccaneers, for whom he started 46 games and recorded 23 sacks.

21. The New Orleans Saints (1980), Dallas Cowboys ('89), New England Patriots ('90), Indianapolis Colts ('91), and New York Jets ('96).

22. George Plimpton—who later was portrayed by Alan Alda in a movie bearing the same title.

23. Smith, who'd had a disappointing season—for him— with 1,204 rushing yards and a 3.7-yard rushing average.

24. Billy Sims, who went on to rush for 5,106 yards and 42 touchdowns in his five-year NFL career, all with the Lions.

25. Tom Dempsey of the New Orleans Saints, who boomed the kick on the last play of a 19–17 defeat of the Detroit Lions.

26. The four, in order: owner Wellington Mara, coach Don Shula, center Mike Webster, and cornerback Mike Haynes.

27. The Pittsburgh Steelers, with whom Mills totaled 127 receptions for 2,003 yards and 15 touchdowns, plus 76 kickoff returns for 1,753 yards (23.1-yard average).

28. The five, in order: coach Joe Gibbs, tackle Dan Dierdorf, defensive back Mel Renfro, tackle/guard Lou Creekmur, and wide receiver Charlie Joiner.

29. Bob Whitfield, who played at Stanford and has been a full-time starter for the Falcons since 1993.

30. Eric Swann of the Arizona Cardinals, a defensive tackle who was selected in the first round (number six overall) by the Cardinals franchise when it was in Phoenix. The two-time Pro Bowler has fared far better than Sitko, who played parts of three seasons in the NFL, none with the team that drafted him.

31. The Buffalo Bills, for whom he was a five-time Pro Bowler (1980–83, '88).

32. Rashaan Salaam of the Chicago Bears, who rushed for 2,055 yards and 24 touchdowns as a junior at the University of Colorado before entering the NFL draft.

33. West Virginia, where he ran for 1,145 yards and six touchdowns as a senior in 1992 and was named team most valuable player.

34. The San Diego Chargers (1988–93), with whom he had 374 receptions for 5,582 yards and 37 touchdowns and played in four Pro Bowls, and the Denver Broncos (1994–96), with whom he had 175 receptions for 2,921 yards and 22 TDs and played in one Pro Bowl.

35. Jim Breech, who made 225 of 313 field goals (.719) in his Bengals career.

36. The Cleveland Browns, who were 12–14–1 under Carson and 1–6 under Shofner.

37. The Denver Broncos, who were 34–33–3 with no postseason appearances under Ralston.

38. Lydell Mitchell, with 5,487 yards from 1972 to 1977.

39. Four-time Pro Bowl running back Roger Craig, who had 66 receptions in 1987 (to Rice's 65) and 76 in '88 (to Rice's 65). Rice, of course, managed to do a little more with his catches: He had 1,078 receiving yards and a league-leading 22 touchdown receptions in '87 (to Craig's 492 yards and one TD), and 1,306 yards and nine TDs in '88 (to Craig's 534 yards and one TD).

40. Barry Word, who led his team that day to a 43–24 home defeat of the Detroit Lions.

41. Larry Csonka, a Hall-of-Famer, with 6,737 yards from 1968 to 1974 and '79.

42. Two. Running back Franco Harris and wide receiver Lynn Swann each won the honor once.

43. The New York Giants, with whom he played in nine Pro Bowls and was named the NFL's lineman of the year in 1956.

44. The Miami Dolphins, by a 14–7 score over the Washington Redskins.

45. The Los Angeles Rams, with whom Cromwell totaled 37 interceptions and eight touchdowns—including three rushing TDs on only seven career carries—in 161 games played.

46. Luwynn.

47. Joe Stydahar (1950–52), Hamp Pool (1952–54), and Sid Gillman (1955–59).

48. The Kansas City Chiefs, with whom he earned all-league notice nine times, had 25 interceptions, and scored eight touchdowns.

49. Twenty-three (1969–91), over which the Steelers were 209–156–1 and won four Super Bowls.

50. Jones, with 886 yards in 1985, 903 yards in '86, and 342 yards in '87. James led the team with 552 yards in '88; Bussey was the Lions' leader all the way back in 1978 (924 yards) and '79 (625).

CROSSING ROUTES

(50 questions, 15 yards each)

1. Name the AFC West running back who led the NFL in rushing in 1989.
2. Name the two players whose jersey numbers were retired by the New York Jets. (Hint: Both are Hall-of-Famers.)
3. How many NFL seasons did Hall of Fame running back Jim Brown play?
4. Of the following Hall of Fame running backs, who is the oldest: Earl Campbell, Tony Dorsett, Walter Payton, or John Riggins?
5. What lineman did the Indianapolis Colts select with the number one overall pick in the 1992 NFL draft?
6. George Blanda set a still-standing NFL record for most interceptions thrown in a season in 1962, when he played for the Houston Oilers. How many did he throw: 32, 37, 42, or 47?
7. What jersey number does Detroit Lions wide receiver Herman Moore wear?
8. Mike Tice played for the Seattle Seahawks (1981–88, 1990–91), Washington Redskins ('89), and Minnesota Vikings (1992–93, '95); John Tice played for the New Orleans Saints (1983–92). What same position did both brothers play?

9. What pass-happy team led the NFL in first downs each season from 1980 to 1983?

10. In 1997 Denver Broncos quarterback John Elway moved into second place on the NFL's all-time list in completions, attempts, and passing yards. Name the Hall-of-Famer Elway surpassed in all three categories.

11. Since the NFL adopted its current overtime system in 1974, what's the most consecutive games a team has played without going to overtime: 48, 110, or 156?

12. What is the name of the Keyshawn Johnson autobiography that was released in 1997, in which the New York Jets wide receiver raised controversy by criticizing teammates and coaches?

13. Who coached the Detroit Lions from 1978 to 1984?

14. When Green Bay Packers running back Dorsey Levens rushed for 1,435 yards in 1997, whose team single-season rushing record did he fall 39 yards short of?

15. Name the Kansas City Chiefs quarterback who threw for a team-record and AFC-best 4,348 yards in 1983.

16. Who is the New England Patriots' all-time leader in receptions and receiving yards?

17. Which NFL team in 1995 became the first to boast a 4,000-yard passer, a 1,000-yard rusher, and more than one 1,000-yard receiver in the same season?

18. Who holds the NFL record for touchdown receptions in a season, with 22?

19. How many 100-yard rushing games did Walter Payton have in his Hall of Fame career: 57, 77, 97, or 107?

20. Name the Hall of Fame kicker who played for the Kansas City Chiefs from 1967 to 1979, the Green Bay Packers from 1980 to 1983, and the Minnesota Vikings from 1984 to 1985.

21. Which of the following NFL coaches holds an undergraduate degree in education: the New Orleans Saints' Mike Ditka, the San Francisco 49ers' Steve Mariucci, the New York Jets' Bill Parcells, or the Philadelphia Eagles' Ray Rhodes?

22. What's the last name of the following NFL brothers: Earl, a wide receiver/tight end who played for the Chicago Bears (1971–73), St. Louis Cardinals (1974–75), and Houston Oilers ('76); Jimmy, a running back/wide receiver who played for the San Francisco 49ers (1969–73); and Mike, a running back who played for the Washington Redskins (1975–78) and San Diego Chargers (1979–80)?

23. Who coached the Green Bay Packers from 1975–83?

24. Against what NFC West foe does San Francisco 49ers wide receiver Jerry Rice have the most career receptions (140), receiving yards (2,150), and touchdown catches (22)?

25. Hall-of-Famer Gene Upshaw has a younger brother who played on the defensive lines of the Cleveland Browns (1968–69), Kansas City Chiefs (1970–75), and St. Louis Cardinals ('76). What's his name: Alvin, Marvin, or Stephen?

26. What Hall of Fame fullback set a still-standing NFL single-game record in 1929 when he scored 40 points in a 40–6 Chicago Cardinals win over the Chicago Bears?

27. Before they defeated the New England Patriots in Super Bowl XXXI, when was the last time the Green Bay Packers made it to the Super Bowl?

28. What are the first names of both of the Bahr brothers, the placekickers who between them played 31 NFL seasons in the 1970s, '80s, and '90s?

29. In what football-rich state was Don Shula, the NFL's all-time winningest coach, born?

30. Name the player who, by the time he retired after

the 1993 season, had set an NFL record for punt returns with 292. (Hint: He played for, in order, the St. Louis Cardinals, Phoenix Cardinals, Green Bay Packers, and Philadelphia Eagles.)

31. How many receptions did San Francisco 49ers wide receiver Jerry Rice, the NFL's number one career pass-catcher in nearly every statistical category, tally as a rookie in 1985: 39, 49, 59, or 69?

32. Where did Hall of Fame halfback Paul Hornung play in college?

33. The Pro Football Hall of Fame Class of 1994 consists of six men: one affiliated with the Minnesota Vikings; one with the Cleveland Browns; one with the San Francisco 49ers; one with the Dallas Cowboys; one with the Cowboys and Denver Broncos; and one with the St. Louis Cardinals and Cowboys. Name any of the six.

34. What coach nicknamed "Red" led the Denver Broncos from 1977 to 1980?

35. What was the name of the NFL team in Milwaukee from 1922 to 1926: Badgers, Bulldogs, Maroons, or Rangers?

36. In 1983 the top five rushers in the AFC played for the Seattle Seahawks, Houston Oilers, Cleveland Browns, Buffalo Bills, and Baltimore Colts. Name any three of them.

37. Who holds the NFL's single-season record for points scored? (Hint: He did it in 1960.)

38. Who is the New England Patriots' career rushing leader: Don Calhoun, Tony Collins, Sam Cunningham, or Jim Nance?

39. Who is the only coach ever to win championships in both the AFL and the NFL?

40. What was the name of the NFL team in Dayton from 1920 to 1929: Red Jackets, Tornadoes, Triangles, or Yellow Jackets?

41. What current NFL team represents the oldest continuing operation in pro football, dating all the way back to 1899?

42. What is the most career safeties any NFL player has had: four, five, six, or seven?

43. What is the most field goals of 50 yards or more one player has kicked in an NFL season: five, six, seven, or eight?

44. What former running back holds the NFL career record for most 200-yard rushing games, with six: Jim Brown, Earl Campbell, Eric Dickerson, or O.J. Simpson?

45. Who holds the all-time NFL record for all-purpose yards in a single game, with 404? (Hint: He played in the AFC West when he set the mark in 1995.)

46. What former Washington Redskins running back carried the ball an NFL-record 45 times in a 20–17 loss at the Cincinnati Bengals in 1988?

47. In 1991 the top five rushers in the NFC played for the Dallas Cowboys, Detroit Lions, New York Giants, Washington Redskins, and Minnesota Vikings. Name any four of them.

48. What team won Super Bowl XI on January 9, 1977?

49. Who is the only player ever to lead the NFL in touchdown passes in four different seasons: Sid Luckman, Dan Marino, Y.A. Tittle, or Johnny Unitas?

50. In how many seasons did former San Francisco 49ers and Kansas City Chiefs quarterback Joe Montana throw for at least 3,000 yards: two, four, six, or eight?

ANSWERS

1. Christian Okoye of the Kansas City Chiefs, with 1,480 yards (10 yards more than the NFC's leader— a Detroit Lions rookie named Barry Sanders—rushed for).

2. Don Maynard (number 13) and Joe Namath (number 12).

3. Nine (1957–65), all with the Cleveland Browns.

4. Riggins, who was born August 4, 1949, in Seneca, Kansas. Dorsett was born April 7, 1954, in Rochester, Pennsylvania; Payton July 25, 1954, in Columbia, Mississippi; and Campbell, March 29, 1955, in Tyler, Texas.

5. Defensive tackle Steve Emtman of the University of Washington.

6. Forty-two.

7. Number 84.

8. Tight end.

9. The San Diego Chargers, with their highest season total in that stretch—379 first downs, only eight off the all-time mark later set by the 1984 Miami Dolphins—coming in 1981.

10. Fran Tarkenton of the Minnesota Vikings (1961–66 and 1972–78) and New York Giants (1967–71), who at his retirement held NFL records with 6,467 attempts, 3,686 completions, and 47,003 yards.

11. The St. Louis (and later Phoenix) Cardinals played 110 straight games without going to overtime. The streak started with a 10–10 tie at the Philadelphia Eagles in December 1986 and ended with a 30–27 win at the Seattle Seahawks in December '93. Ironically, the team has played at least two overtime games in every season since (through '97).

12. *Just Give Me the Damn Ball: The Fast Times and Hard Knocks of an NFL Rookie.* (*Just Give Me the Damn Ball* is an acceptable answer.)

13. Monte Clark, under whom the Lions were 43–63–1 and won the NFC Central in 1983.

14. Jim Taylor's. The Hall of Fame fullback set the mark of 1,474 yards in 1962, when he led the NFL in rushing yards and touchdowns (19).

15. Bill Kenney, who played from 1979 to 1988 with the team and totaled 17,277 passing yards.

16. Stanley Morgan, who caught 534 passes for 10,352 yards with the team from 1977 to 1989.

17. The Atlanta Falcons, thanks to Jeff George's 4,143 yards passing and Craig Heyward's 1,083 yards rushing, and the receiving yardage of Eric Metcalf (1,189), Terance Mathis (1,039), and Bert Emanuel (1,039).

18. Jerry Rice of the San Francisco 49ers, who accomplished the feat in 1987.

19. Payton had 77, an NFL record.

20. Jan Stenerud, who had 1,699 points (373 field goals, 580 extra points) in his 19-year AFL and NFL career.

21. Parcells, who earned the degree from Wichita State in 1964.

22. Thomas.

23. Bart Starr, the Hall of Fame Packers quarterback, under whom the team was 53–77–3 with one post-season appearance (in 1982).

24. The Atlanta Falcons.

25. Marvin. The younger Upshaw played in 99 games and had the career highlight of a 52-yard interception return for a touchdown in 1974.

26. Ernie Nevers, who scored the points on six rushing touchdowns—also a record—and four extra-point kicks. The 40 points and six rushing TDs are the NFL's longest-standing records to date.

27. The 1967 Packers hammered the Oakland Raiders 33–14 in Super Bowl II on January 14, 1968, in Miami.

28. Chris and Matt. Chris Bahr kicked for the Cincinnati Bengals (1976–79), Oakland/Los Angeles Raiders (1980–88), and San Diego Chargers ('89); Matt Bahr kicked for the Pittsburgh Steelers (1979–80), San Francisco 49ers ('81), Cleveland Browns (1981–89), New York Giants (1990–92), Philadelphia Eagles ('93), and New England Patriots (1993–95).

29. Ohio (Painesville).

30. Vai Sikahema, whose record was surpassed in 1996 by both the Oakland Raiders' Tim Brown and the New England Patriots' Dave Meggett.

31. Forty-nine (in 16 games).

32. Notre Dame.

33. The six, in order: coach Bud Grant, running back Leroy Kelly, cornerback Jimmy Johnson, defensive tackle Randy White, running back Tony Dorsett, and tight end Jackie Smith.

34. Robert "Red" Miller, under whom the Broncos were 42–25, reached the postseason three times, and played in one Super Bowl.

35. Badgers. Milwaukee compiled a 16–27–6 record before NFL commissioner Joe Carr decided prior to the 1927 season to eliminate the league's financially weaker teams and consolidate its best players.

36. The five, in order: Curt Warner (1,449 yards), Earl Campbell (1,301), Mike Pruitt (1,184), Joe Cribbs (1,131), and Curtis Dickey (1,122).

37. Paul Hornung of the Green Bay Packers, with 176. Hornung, who played halfback and kicker and is in the Hall of Fame, scored the points on 15 touchdowns, 15 field goals, and 41 extra-point kicks.

38. Cunningham, with 5,453 yards from 1973 to 1979 and 1981 to 1982. Nance (1965–71) is second with

5,323, Collins (1981–87) third with 4,647, and Calhoun fifth (behind Curtis Martin) with 3,391.

39. Hall-of-Famer Weeb Ewbank, whose Baltimore Colts won the NFL championship in 1958 and whose New York Jets won the AFL championship (before going on to defeat the Colts in the Super Bowl) in '68.

40. Triangles. Unfortunately, the Triangles compiled a record of only 18–51–8 before being purchased by a pair of New Yorkers and moved to Brooklyn, where they became the Dodgers.

41. The Arizona Cardinals. In 1899, a Chicagoan named Chris O'Brien formed a neighborhood team on the city's South Side called the Morgan Athletic Club; the team later became known as the Normals, then the Racine (for a street in Chicago) Cardinals, the Chicago Cardinals, the St. Louis Cardinals, the Phoenix Cardinals, and, in '94, the Arizona Cardinals.

42. Four, by two players: Hall of Fame linebacker Ted Hendricks and former defensive tackle Doug English.

43. Eight, by the Atlanta Falcons' Morten Andersen in 1995. The distances: 59, 55, 55, 54, 52, 51, 51, and 50.

44. Simpson. Brown and Campbell each had four; Dickerson had three.

45. Glyn Milburn, then of the Denver Broncos, who set the mark in a 31–27 loss at home to the Seattle Seahawks. For the game, Milburn had 131 rushing yards, 45 receiving yards, 133 kickoff-return yards, and 95 punt-return yards.

46. Jamie Morris.

47. The five, in order: Emmitt Smith (1,563 yards), Barry Sanders (1,548), Rodney Hampton (1,059), Earnest Byner (1,048), and Herschel Walker (825).

48. The Oakland Raiders, by a 32–14 score over the Minnesota Vikings.
49. Unitas, who did it with the Baltimore Colts each season from 1957 to 1960. Luckman, Marino, and Tittle all did it three times.
50. Eight: in 1981, 1983–85, 1987, and 1989–90 with the 49ers, and in 1994 with the Chiefs.

POST PATTERNS

(50 questions, 20 yards each)

1. There have been two 99-yard touchdown passes in the NFL in the 1990s. Name the thrower *and* the receiver on either one of the hook-ups.

2. The 1983 Green Bay Packers hold the NFL record for most overtime games played in one season, with how many?

3. In a 1967 game against the Pittsburgh Steelers, St. Louis Cardinals kicker Jim Bakken set an NFL record that still stands for most field-goal attempts in one game. How many did Bakken try?

4. Mike Michalske, who starred for the Green Bay Packers' NFL championship teams of 1929, '30, '31, and '35, was the first player at his position enshrined in the Pro Football Hall of Fame. What position did Michalske play?

5. Name the Hall of Fame running back who has the best per-carry average (minimum 750 attempts) in NFL history.

6. If an official touches the top of his cap with the palm of his right hand, what is he signaling?

7. Who holds the NFL career postseason record for most rushing attempts?

8. What jersey number does Tampa Bay Buccaneers running back Warrick Dunn wear?

9. Who coached the New Orleans Saints from their inception in 1967 through the seventh game of 1970?

10. How many times from 1990 to 1997 did the Tampa Bay Buccaneers finish in last place in the NFC Central?

11. How many points did the 2–14 Seattle Seahawks score in 1992: 140, 190, 240, or 290?

12. Name the Dallas Cowboys linebacker who earned most valuable player honors in the team's 16–13 loss to the Miami Dolphins in Super Bowl V.

13. Name either of the starting wide receivers for the Carolina Panthers in the 1996 NFC Championship Game.

14. What team did the Cleveland Browns defeat 23–20 in two overtimes in a 1986 AFC divisional playoff game, the last NFL game to reach a second extra session?

15. Before what season did the NFL Colts move from Baltimore to Indianapolis?

16. What three NFL quarterbacks threw for more than 4,000 yards in 1996?

17. Where did Hall of Fame quarterback Bob Griese play in college?

18. Where did Hall of Fame running back Franco Harris play in college?

19. With what team did Hall of Fame halfback Doak Walker play his entire NFL career?

20. Which one of the following NFLers holds a degree in accounting: Arizona Cardinals cornerback Aeneas Williams, Denver Broncos defensive end Alfred Williams, Dallas Cowboys offensive tackle Erik Williams, or Seattle Seahawks cornerback Willie Williams?

21. What team won Super Bowl VIII on January 13, 1974?

22. What is former NFL star running back Bo Jackson's actual first name?

23. Name any two of the three last-place teams in the NFC in 1993.

24. Who coached the Chicago Bears from 1978 to 1981 before being replaced by Mike Ditka?

25. Name the longtime AFC head coach who also held the reins over teams in both the Canadian Football League and the United States Football League.

26. What quarterback was the first player selected in the NFL expansion draft in 1995?

27. Who was the first player to catch more than 100 passes in a single NFL season? (Hint: He accomplished the feat in 1984.)

28. Since the NFL-AFL merger prior to the 1970 season, how many division championships have been won by the New York Jets?

29. Which player in 1995 set an NFL single-season record for 100-yard receiving games, with 11: the St. Louis Rams' Isaac Bruce, the Dallas Cowboys' Michael Irvin, the Detroit Lions' Herman Moore, or the San Francisco 49ers' Jerry Rice?

30. Name the Hall of Fame fullback who owns the NFL single-game record for highest average rushing gain (minimum 10 attempts), with 17.09. (Hint: He accomplished the feat in 1950.)

31. Of the following former or current running backs, who had the most rushing touchdowns in his rookie NFL season: the Los Angeles Rams' Eric Dickerson (1983), the New England Patriots' Curtis Martin ('95), the Detroit Lions' Barry Sanders ('89), or the Cincinnati Bengals' Ickey Woods ('88)?

32. Eric Dickerson had one-season stints with what two

teams in the final two years (1992 and '93) of his NFL career?

33. How many 1,000-yard rushing seasons did Hall-of-Famer Walter Payton have in his 13-year NFL career?

34. What former Miami Dolphins kicker holds the NFL single-season record for most extra points, with 66? (Hint: He played with the team for his entire six-year career, from 1979 to 1984.)

35. Who was the first sitting United States President to attend an NFL game?

36. Name the Los Angeles Rams kicker who was a perfect 17-for-17 in field goals in 1991.

37. For how many consecutive NFL seasons (through 1997) has the Detroit Lions' Barry Sanders rushed for at least 1,000 yards?

38. How many losing seasons does Marty Schottenheimer have in his 14-year NFL head coaching career (through 1997)?

39. With what two NFL teams has Arizona Cardinals coach Vince Tobin served as defensive coordinator?

40. Name any three of the six last-place teams in the NFL in the 15-game 1987 season.

41. What was Dave Wannstedt's first season as coach of the Chicago Bears?

42. Which one of the following star running backs was not voted the NFL's offensive rookie of the year: Jerome Bettis, Terrell Davis, Marshall Faulk, or Barry Sanders?

43. With what United States Football League team did defensive end Reggie White play in 1984 and '85?

44. Name any two of the three teams defensive end Sean Jones starred for in his 13-year NFL career, which ended in 1996.

45. What team won Super Bowl IV on January 11, 1970?

46. In descriptions of defenses, what do designations such as "4–3" and "3–4" mean?

47. What center played in 245 games with the Atlanta Falcons from 1969 to 1986?

48. What current NFLer won the Davey O'Brien Trophy as the nation's best collegiate quarterback in 1988?

49. How many times was former Minnesota Vikings tight end Steve Jordan—who played for the team from 1982 to 1994 and totaled 498 receptions for 6,307 yards and 28 touchdowns—voted to the Pro Bowl: none, two, four, or six?

50. The Pro Football Hall of Fame Class of 1992 consists of four men: one affiliated with the Detroit Lions; one with the Baltimore Colts and San Diego Chargers; one with the New York Jets and Washington Redskins; and one with the Oakland and Los Angeles Raiders. Name any of the four.

ANSWERS

1. San Diego Chargers quarterback Stan Humphries to wide receiver Tony Martin against the Seattle Seahawks in '94, and Green Bay Packers quarterback Brett Favre to wide receiver Robert Brooks against the Chicago Bears in '95.

2. Five. They beat the Houston Oilers 41–38 and the Tampa Bay Buccaneers 12–9, and lost to the Minnesota Vikings 20–17, the Detroit Lions 23–20, and the Atlanta Falcons 47–41.

3. Nine. Bakken made seven of those—also a record, but one he shares with former Minnesota Vikings kicker Rich Karlis and former Dallas Cowboys

kicker Chris Boniol—and St. Louis won the game 28–14.

4. Offensive guard.

5. Jim Brown of the Cleveland Browns, with 5.22 yards a carry.

6. Ineligible receiver (or ineligible member of the kicking team) downfield.

7. Hall-of-Famer Franco Harris, who had 400 carries in 19 postseason games with the Pittsburgh Steelers.

8. Number 28.

9. Tom Fears, who led the Saints to a 13–34–2 record before being fired.

10. Four: in 1991 (3–13), '93 (5–11), '94 (6–10), and '95 (7–9).

11. The Seahawks scored 140 points, an astonishingly low 8.75 a game—and a full 65 points less than the output of the 2–14 New England Patriots, the next-lowest-scoring NFL team that season.

12. Chuck Howley.

13. Mark Carrier and Willie Green. Carrier, who had started 15 games in the regular season, caught four passes for 65 yards in the 30–13 loss at the Green Bay Packers; Green, who'd started 10 games, caught five passes for 51 yards.

14. The New York Jets, at 17:02 of overtime when the Browns' Mark Moseley kicked a 27-yard field goal to cap a comeback from a 20–10 fourth-quarter deficit.

15. The Colts opened play in Indianapolis in 1984.

16. Mark Brunell of the Jacksonville Jaguars (4,367), Vinny Testaverde of the Baltimore Ravens (4,177), and Drew Bledsoe of the New England Patriots (4,086).

17. Purdue.

18. Penn State.

19. The Detroit Lions, from 1950 to 1955.

20. Aeneas Williams, who earned it from Southern University in 1990.

21. The Miami Dolphins, by a 24–7 score over the Minnesota Vikings.

22. Vincent.

23. The 4–12 Washington Redskins (NFC East), 5–11 Tampa Bay Buccaneers (NFC Central), and 5–11 Los Angeles Rams (NFC West).

24. Neill Armstrong, under whom the Bears were 30–35 with one postseason appearance (1979).

25. Marv Levy of the Kansas City Chiefs and Buffalo Bills, who coached the CFL's Montreal Alouettes from 1973 to 1977 and the USFL's Chicago Blitz in '84.

26. Steve Beuerlein, by the Jacksonville Jaguars. Ironically, Beuerlein later became a member of the other expansion team from that year, the Carolina Panthers.

27. Art Monk of the Washington Redskins, with 106. Two AFL players reached the 100–reception mark years earlier: Lionel Taylor of the Denver Broncos, who had exactly 100 catches in 1961, and Charley Hennigan of the Houston Oilers, who had 101 in '64.

28. None. The Jets won the AFL East in 1968 and '69, but they've never won the AFC East.

29. Irvin. Although Rice (1,848), Bruce (1,781), and Moore (1,686) all had more receiving yards than Irvin (1,603), it was the Cowboys star who had the most 100-yard games.

30. Marion Motley of the Cleveland Browns, who had 188 yards on only 11 carries in a 45–7 Browns win.

31. Dickerson, with an NFL rookie-record 18. Woods had 15, and Martin (who's now with the Jets) and Sanders had 14 apiece.

32. The Los Angeles Raiders, whom he led in rushing in 1992 with 729 yards, and the Atlanta Falcons, with

whom he had the last 91 yards of his career in '93.

33. Ten. The Chicago Bears great failed to reach the mark in his rookie season (1975) and his final season ('87), and in the strike-shortened '82 season.

34. Uwe von Schamann, who accomplished the feat in 1984.

35. Lyndon B. Johnson, who took in a Washington Redskins-Baltimore Colts exhibition opener at D.C. Stadium in 1966.

36. Tony Zendejas.

37. Nine, an NFL record—and exactly as many NFL seasons as he's played.

38. None. Schottenheimer had .500 records with the Cleveland Browns in 1984 and '85, but in three more years with the Browns and the past nine with the Kansas City Chiefs, the worst one of his teams has finished is 8–7–1.

39. The Chicago Bears (1986–92) and Indianapolis Colts (1994–95).

40. The 6–9 New York Jets (AFC East), 4–11 Cincinnati Bengals (AFC Central), 4–11 Kansas City Chiefs (AFC West), 6–9 New York Giants (NFC East), 4–11 Detroit Lions (NFC Central), and 3–12 Atlanta Falcons (NFC West).

41. Wannstedt's first season was 1993, when the Bears were 7–9.

42. Davis, of the Denver Broncos—even though he rushed for 1,117 yards and seven touchdowns as a rookie in 1995. He was passed over in favor of New England Patriots running back Curtis Martin, who rushed for 1,487 yards and 14 TDs that season.

43. The Memphis Showboats, with whom White started all 34 games he played in and totaled 23.5 sacks.

44. The Los Angeles Raiders (1984–87), with whom he started 32 games and had 31 sacks; the Houston Oilers (1988–93), with whom he started 64 games and

had 57.5 sacks; and the Green Bay Packers (1994–96), with whom he started 47 games and had 24.5 sacks.

45. The Kansas City Chiefs, by a 23–7 score over the Minnesota Vikings.

46. Using the "4–3" as an example—and speaking very generally—the first figure (the "4") refers to the number of linemen, and the second figure (the "3") to the number of linebackers.

47. Jeff Van Note, who spent his entire career with the Falcons and played his final season at the age of 40.

48. Troy Aikman of the Dallas Cowboys, who was in his senior season at UCLA.

49. Six: every season from 1986 to 1991.

50. The four, in order: cornerback Lem Barney, tight end John Mackey, running back John Riggins, and team/league administrator Al Davis.

BREAKAWAY RUNS

(25 questions, 30 yards each)

1. Which one of the following Hall of Fame quarterbacks was an Ivy Leaguer: Sammy Baugh, Otto Graham, Sonny Jurgensen, or Sid Luckman?
2. What is New York Jets coach Bill Parcells's real first name?
3. Which official keeps track of the time in an NFL game: the back judge, the field judge, the line judge, or the side judge?
4. Of the following former Minnesota Vikings—all from the four-Super Bowl era of the 1960s and '70s—which *three* are in the Pro Football Hall of Fame: defensive end Carl Eller, coach Bud Grant, safety Paul Krause, defensive end Jim Marshall, defensive tackle Alan Page, quarterback Fran Tarkenton, center Mick Tingelhoff, and offensive tackle Ron Yary?
5. The NFL record for average regular-season paid attendance (all teams) was set in 1995, at what figure: 62,682, 65,402, 68,388, or 71,448?
6. Who is the New York Giants' all-time interceptions leader? (Hint: He's a Hall-of-Famer.)
7. Where did Hall of Fame running back Larry Csonka play in college?

8. Name the Hall-of-Famer who played defensive tackle for the San Francisco 49ers from 1950 to 1963. (Hint: He was born in Italy.)

9. In 1990 the Chicago Bears won the NFC Central title with an 11–5 record, while the Detroit Lions, Green Bay Packers, Minnesota Vikings, and Tampa Bay Buccaneers all finished 6–10. What was the official order of finish (based on the NFL's tiebreaker system) in the division?

10. What team did the Tampa Bay Buccaneers defeat 24–17 at home in the 1979 NFC divisional playoffs in their first-ever postseason game?

11. Of the following Hall of Fame quarterbacks, who threw for the most touchdown passes as a pro: George Blanda, Terry Bradshaw, Len Dawson, or Sonny Jurgensen?

12. Nose tackle Greg Kragen played the first nine seasons of his NFL career (1985–93) with the Denver Broncos and the last three (1995–97) with the Carolina Panthers. With what AFC West team did he play in '94?

13. Detroit Lions coach Bobby Ross had three college head coaching jobs before jumping to the NFL in 1992. Name any two of them.

14. Name the Hall of Fame safety who played for the Green Bay Packers from 1960 to 1971.

15. What team did the Dallas Cowboys defeat 23–6 in the 1977 NFC Championship Game to advance to Super Bowl XII?

16. In 1949, the NFL had two 1,000-yard rushers for the first time ever. Name either one of them. (Hint: Both are Hall-of-Famers.)

17. From his rookie year of 1985 through the '97 season, how many times did Buffalo Bills defensive end Bruce Smith lead the NFL in sacks?

18. Name both teams three-time Pro Bowl running back

Chuck Muncie played for during his nine-year NFL career (1976–84).

19. Who holds the Miami Dolphins' single-season rushing record?

20. What AFL team selected Illinois running back Jim Grabowski in 1966 with its first-ever draft pick?

21. What team in 1983 set the NFL record for most points scored in a season, with 541?

22. Carolina Panthers coach Dom Capers previously served as an assistant coach with what two NFL teams?

23. Which was the NFL's only winless team (0–8–1) in the strike-shortened 1982 season?

24. The Pro Football Hall of Fame Class of 1990 consists of seven men: one affiliated with the Dallas Cowboys; one with the Kansas City Chiefs; one with the Miami Dolphins; one with the San Francisco 49ers; one with the Pittsburgh Steelers; one with the Steelers and Seattle Seahawks; and one with the Baltimore Colts, Green Bay Packers, and Oakland Raiders. Name any one of them.

25. What AFC Central team drafted Tulsa wide receiver Stave Largent in the fourth round of the 1976 draft?

ANSWERS

1. Luckman, who played for the Chicago Bears from 1939 to 1950 after graduating from Columbia. Baugh, who played for the Washington Redskins from 1937 to 1952, went to Texas Christian; Graham, who played for the Cleveland Browns from 1946 to 1955, went to Northwestern; and Jurgensen, who played for the Philadelphia Eagles from 1957 to

1963 and the Redskins from 1964 to 1974, went to Duke.

2. Duane, as in Duane Charles Parcells—a far cry from "Bill." Then again, for a guy nicknamed "Tuna," that doesn't seem so strange, does it?

3. The line judge.

4. Grant (inducted in 1994), Page ('88), and Tarkenton ('86).

5. The record still stands at 62,682.

6. Emlen Tunnell, who had 74 in 11 seasons (1948–58) with the team. Tunnell, a safety who played his final three seasons (1959–61) with the Green Bay Packers, totaled 79 pickoffs for his career.

7. Syracuse.

8. Leo Nomellini, who didn't miss a single game in his career and played in 10 Pro Bowls.

9. Tampa Bay, Detroit, Green Bay, and Minnesota. The Buccaneers finished in second place because of their 5–1 record in games involving those teams.

10. The Philadelphia Eagles.

11. Jurgensen, with 255, followed by Dawson (239), Blanda (236), and Bradshaw (212).

12. The Kansas City Chiefs, with whom he started only two games and had no sacks.

13. The Citadel (1973–77), the University of Maryland (1982–86), and Georgia Tech (1987–91).

14. Willie Wood, who had 48 interceptions in his career and competed in six NFL championship games, including Super Bowls I and II.

15. The Minnesota Vikings.

16. The two: Steve Van Buren of the Philadelphia Eagles, who had a league- and career-high 1,146 yards in 1949 and was inducted into the Hall of Fame in 1965; and Tony Canadeo of the Green Bay Packers, who had a career-high 1,052 yards in '49 and was inducted in '74.

17. Zero—a hard-to-believe fact, considering Smith's 154 career sacks through 1997 placed him second on the all-time NFL list (behind Reggie White's 176.5). In fact, only once had Smith led the AFC in sacks: in '97, when he had 14. Smith also tied (with the Seattle Seahawks' Michael McCrary) for the AFC lead in '96 with 13.5.

18. The New Orleans Saints (1976–80) and the San Diego Chargers (1980–84). Muncie finished his career with 1,561 carries for 6,702 yards and 71 touchdowns, plus 263 receptions for 2,323 yards and three more TDs.

19. Delvin Williams, with 1,258 yards in 1978.

20. The Miami Dolphins. Unfortunately, Grabowski also was drafted by the Green Bay Packers; he signed with the NFL club and never played a down for the Dolphins.

21. The Washington Redskins, who didn't come close to their regular-season average of 33.8 points in losing 38–9 to the Los Angeles Raiders in Super Bowl XVIII.

22. The New Orleans Saints as defensive backs coach (1986–91) and the Pittsburgh Steelers as defensive coordinator (1992–94).

23. The Baltimore Colts.

24. The seven, in order: coach Tom Landry, defensive tackle Buck Buchanan, quarterback Bob Griese, tackle Bob St. Clair, linebacker Jack Lambert, running back Franco Harris, and linebacker Ted Hendricks.

25. The Houston Oilers, who must not have seen the Hall of Fame in Largent's future when they traded him in training camp to the Seattle Seahawks for an eighth-round pick in the 1977 draft (with which they would select Georgia wide receiver Steve Davis).

BOMBS AWAY

(25 questions, 50 yards each)

1. Which team lost 23–21 to the Minnesota Vikings on November 5, 1989, in the only NFL overtime game ever decided by a safety?
2. Name either of the two players who combined on an NFL-record 104-yard interception return for the Philadelphia Eagles in a 1996 defeat of the Dallas Cowboys.
3. Name the teams that had the NFL's highest and lowest home attendance totals in 1996.
4. Name any two of the three NFL teams Hall of Fame defensive end Doug Atkins played for.
5. In what city was San Francisco 49ers quarterback Steve Young born?
6. Name the two head coaches who in 1992 returned to NFL teams they'd coached before.
7. Name the pair of linebackers the Dallas Cowboys selected in the first round of the 1975 draft. (Hint: Though both went on to star with the team, one did it as a defensive tackle.)
8. Name the man who coached the Green Bay Packers to a 1–10–1 record in 1958—his only season in that job—before being succeeded by Vince Lombardi.
9. Name the coach under whom the Washington Red-

skins were 21–46–3 from 1961 to 1965.

10. How many victories did Don Shula, the NFL's all-time winningest coach, amass in his 33 years in the league? (Hint: It's more than 300 and less than 350.)

11. The Buffalo Bills and St. Louis (formerly Los Angeles) Rams have squared off only seven times in the regular season (through 1997). Who holds the series advantage, and by what count?

12. What is the NFL record for most punt returns by one player in a single game?

13. Name the Hall of Fame safety who holds the NFL career record for interceptions returned for touchdowns, with nine.

14. What was the first expansion team ever to win an NFL championship? (Hint: The team did lose its final game that season.)

15. Where did Hall of Fame running back Gale Sayers play in college?

16. What is the NFL record for most interceptions by both teams in one game?

17. In what city was Green Bay Packers quarterback Brett Favre born?

18. How many receptions did Carolina Panthers star tight end Wesley Walls have in his four seasons (1989–91, '93) with the San Francisco 49ers? (A guess within five receptions of the actual total counts as a correct answer.)

19. Miami Dolphins coach Jimmy Johnson has been an assistant coach in six different college programs. Name any three of them.

20. Name any one of the four members of the Pro Football Hall of Fame class of 1988.

21. Who was the first NFL player to rush for 1,000 yards in a season with two different teams? (Hint: The first of the teams was the San Francisco 49ers.)

22. Name any one of the four NFL teams Hall of Fame

offensive tackle William Roy "Link" Lyman played for.

23. What was the name of the first person to be paid to play football: David "Blip" Benson, William "Pudge" Heffelfinger, Samuel "Mo" Lawrence, or Dick "Buckets" Liberman?

24. How old was the youngest head coach in NFL history?

25. What team on January 1, 1961, won the first AFL championship game?

ANSWERS

1. The Los Angeles Rams, when the Vikes' Mike Merriweather blocked a Dale Hatcher punt out of the end zone.

2. James Willis and Troy Vincent. As Dallas was driving for a potential game-tying field goal or winning touchdown in the final minute of the game in Texas Stadium, Willis, a linebacker, intercepted Troy Aikman in the end zone; Willis then returned the ball to the Eagles' 10-yard line before lateraling to Vincent, who raced 90 yards for a touchdown in a 31–21 win.

3. The Kansas City Chiefs had the highest total, 610,617 (76,327 a game); the Houston Oilers had the lowest total, 254,600 (31,825).

4. The Cleveland Browns (1953–54), Chicago Bears (1955–66), and New Orleans Saints (1967–69).

5. Salt Lake City.

6. The Los Angeles Rams' Chuck Knox and the Indianapolis Colts' Ted Marchibroda. Knox, who had gone 57–20–1 from 1973 to 1977, this time went only 15–33 from 1992 to 1994; Marchibroda, who

had gone 41–36–0 from 1975 to 1979, went 32–35–0 from 1992 to 1995.

7. Maryland's Randy White and Langston (Oklahoma) University's Thomas Henderson. White reached the Hall of Fame as a DT, while Henderson—who became better-known as "Hollywood" Henderson—saw his career cut short by off-the-field problems.

8. Ray "Scooter" McLean.

9. Bill McPeak.

10. Shula won 347 games, including 328 in the regular season (either answer is acceptable). His overall record: 347–173–6.

11. The Bills, by a 4–3 count. The Bills won in 1980, '89, '92, and '95; the Rams won in '70, '74, and '83.

12. Eleven, by Eddie Brown of the Washington Redskins in a 10–0 win at the Tampa Bay Buccaneers in 1977.

13. Ken Houston, who starred for the Houston Oilers from 1967 to 1972 and the Washington Redskins from 1973 to 1980. The 10-time Pro Bowler's 49 career interceptions yielded a staggering 898 return yards, an average of 18.3.

14. The Minnesota Vikings, who began play in 1961 and won the NFL title in 1969, but went on to lose the Super Bowl to the AFL-champion Kansas City Chiefs.

15. The University of Kansas.

16. Thirteen, by the Houston Oilers (eight) and Denver Broncos (five) in a 34–17 Oilers win in 1962.

17. Gulfport, Mississippi. Favre grew up in Kiln, Mississippi, but wasn't born there.

18. Eleven. Walls—who went on to become a Pro Bowler with the Carolina Panthers—had four receptions in 16 games in 1989, five receptions in 16 games in '90, two receptions in 15 games in '91, and no receptions in six games in '93.

19. Louisiana Tech (1965), Wichita State (1967), Iowa

State (1968–69), Oklahoma (1970–72), Arkansas (1973–76), and Pittsburgh (1977–78).

20. Wide receiver Fred Biletnikoff, tight end Mike Ditka, linebacker Jack Ham, and defensive tackle Alan Page.

21. Delvin Williams, who gained 1,203 yards with the 49ers in 1976 and 1,258 yards with the Miami Dolphins in '78. Interestingly, they were the only 1,000-yard performances of his eight-year NFL career.

22. The Canton Bulldogs (1922–23, '25), Cleveland Bulldogs ('24), Frankford Yellow Jackets ('25), and Chicago Bears (1926–28, 1930–31, 1933–34).

23. Heffelfinger, who was paid $500 by the Allegheny (Pennsylvania) Athletic Association to play in a game November 12, 1892, against the Pittsburgh Athletic Club. The only points of the game were scored by Heffelfinger, who recovered a Pittsburgh fumble and returned it 25 yards for a touchdown. (The other names are made up.)

24. Harland Svare was 31 when he took over the Los Angeles Rams nine games into the 1962 season. He went 14–31–3 before being replaced prior to the '66 campaign by George Allen.

25. The Houston Oilers, by a 24–16 score over the Los Angeles Chargers.

FIELD GOALS

INSIDE THE 20

(25 questions)

1. What Los Angeles Raiders player rushed for an all-time "Monday Night Football"-high 221 yards in a 37–14 win at the Seattle Seahawks in 1987? (Hint: His leveling of would-be tackler Brian Bosworth in that game provided one of the greatest highlights in "MNF" history.)
2. Name the only player whose jersey number has been retired by the Seattle Seahawks.
3. What AFC East team did the Pittsburgh Steelers defeat 20–16 at home in the 1995 AFC Championship Game?
4. Which one of the following Hall of Fame quarterbacks did not wear jersey number 12: the Pittsburgh Steelers' Terry Bradshaw, the New York Jets' Joe Namath, the Dallas Cowboys' Roger Staubach, or the Baltimore Colts' Johnny Unitas?
5. Name the only player whose jersey number has been retired by the San Diego Chargers.

6. By what nickname was former Dallas Cowboys star defensive end Ed Jones known?

7. True or false: Since opening play in Baltimore in 1996, the Ravens have never appeared on "Monday Night Football" (through the '97 season).

8. Which one of the following former Cincinnati Bengals draftees was not a first-round pick: quarterback David Klingler, offensive tackle Anthony Muñoz, or defensive tackle Kimo von Oelhoffen?

9. By what name was the facility in which the San Francisco 49ers play their home games known from 1971 to 1994?

10. True or false: Dallas Cowboys wide receiver Michael Irvin played in college at Northwestern.

11. What NFC Central team did the Philadelphia Eagles defeat 58–37 at home in the 1995 NFC wild-card playoffs, in the highest-scoring postseason game in NFL history?

12. What team did the Dallas Cowboys defeat 38–27 at home in the 1995 NFC Championship Game?

13. What jersey number does Detroit Lions quarterback Scott Mitchell wear: number 4 or number 19?

14. In what facility did the Miami Dolphins play their home games from their inception in 1966 through '86?

15. Who was the number one overall pick in the 1998 NFL draft?

16. Who is the only person ever to play in both the Super Bowl and the World Series?

17. Which one of the following former Carolina Panthers draftees was not a first-round pick: wide receiver Rae Carruth, quarterback Kerry Collins, or safety Chad Cota?

18. Name the Dallas Cowboys tight end who dropped a would-be winning pass in the end zone in a Super Bowl loss to the Pittsburgh Steelers.

19. With what team did defensive tackle Dana Stubble-field play the first five seasons of his NFL career (1993–97) before signing as a free agent with the Washington Redskins in 1998?

20. By what nickname was former Houston Oilers and Atlanta Falcons star wide receiver and kick returner Billy Johnson known?

21. Who is the Tennessee Oilers' all-time leader in pass-ing yards and touchdown passes? (Hint: He played with the team only when it was in Houston.)

22. True or false: No Super Bowl ever has gone to over-time.

23. Who is the New Orleans Saints' all-time leader in passing yards and touchdown passes?

24. Which one of the following former Oakland Raiders draftees was not a first-round pick: running back Joe Aska, wide receiver Tim Brown, or cornerback Charles Woodson?

25. By what nickname was former Los Angeles Rams and San Francisco 49ers star linebacker Jack Reyn-olds known: "Anvil," "Hacksaw," "Hammer," or "Hitman"?

20–29 YARDS
(25 questions)

1. In what facility did the Dallas Cowboys play their home games before Texas Stadium was opened in 1971? (Hint: It's always been a great place to be on New Year's Day.)

2. Which one of the following former Dallas Cowboys draftees was not a first-round pick: running back Tony Dorsett, defensive tackle Leon Lett, or defen-sive tackle Russell Maryland?

3. Which team posted the best overall record in the 10-year history of the AFL: the Denver Broncos or the San Diego Chargers?

4. What former San Francisco 49ers coach reached 100 career victories faster than any other coach in NFL history?

5. In what year did the NFL make it mandatory for all teams to display the names of players on their jerseys: 1950, 1970, or 1990?

6. What AFC Central team did the Denver Broncos defeat 23–20 in overtime on the road in the 1986 AFC Championship Game?

7. What team did the Pittsburgh Steelers defeat at home in both the 1978 and '79 AFC Championship Games: the Denver Broncos or the Houston Oilers?

8. Which one of the following former Los Angeles Rams draftees was not a first-round pick: running back Jerome Bettis, defensive tackle Sean Gilbert, or safety Keith Lyle?

9. What jersey number does Tennessee Oilers quarterback Steve McNair wear: number 9, number 12, or number 15?

10. The Washington Redskins set the NFL's all-time playoff high for points in a quarter when they scored how many points in the second quarter of Super Bowl XXII: 21, 35, or 49?

11. Which one of the following former New York Giants draftees was not a first-round pick: quarterback Dave Brown, quarterback Danny Kanell, or linebacker Lawrence Taylor?

12. Where did Hall of Fame running back Walter Payton play in college: Jackson State, Ohio State, or Washington State?

13. Name the teams involved in either of the two 1997 NFL regular-season games that were played to ties.

14. True or false: No player ever has ended an NFL

game by returning the overtime kickoff for a touchdown.

15. With what team did running back Terry Allen spend his first five years in the NFL (1990–94) before signing as a free agent with the Washington Redskins in 1995: the Atlanta Falcons, Chicago Bears, Denver Broncos, or Minnesota Vikings?

16. Entering the 1998 season, only one nonkicker in the history of the NFL had scored at least 1,000 career points. Name him. (Hint: He was still an active player in '98.)

17. What was the first AFL or NFL team to play its home games indoors?

18. At what university did current NFLers Quentin Coryatt, Greg Hill, Leeland McElroy, and Richmond Webb all play?

19. What jersey number does Minnesota Vikings defensive tackle John Randle wear: number 62 or number 93?

20. Name the only player whose jersey number has been retired by the Washington Redskins. (Hint: This quarterback could really "sling" it.)

21. Which one of the following former San Diego Chargers draftees was not a first-round pick: quarterback Ryan Leaf, quarterback Craig Whelihan, or tight end Kellen Winslow?

22. Who is the Cincinnati Bengals' all-time leader in passing yards and touchdown passes? (Hint: It isn't Boomer Esiason.)

23. What's the highest number of receptions an NFL player has ever had in one season without catching a single touchdown pass: 45 or 85?

24. How many total points did the world-champion 1985 Chicago Bears allow in their three playoff games, including the Super Bowl: none, 10 or 27?

25. In 1982, when an NFL players strike abbreviated the

season, how many regular-season games did each team play: six, nine, or 12?

30–39 YARDS
(25 questions)

1. True or false: Running back Marcus Allen never played for the *Oakland* Raiders.
2. True or false: Hall-of-Famer O.J. Simpson's single-game career-high of 273 yards rushing—the NFL's second-highest total ever—was set in a Thanksgiving Day game.
3. What AFC East team did the Buffalo Bills defeat 29–10 on the road in the 1992 AFC Championship Game?
4. True or false: Since opening play in Baltimore in 1996, the Ravens have a winning record in regular-season games against NFC opponents (through the '97 season).
5. Which one of the following former Washington Redskins draftees was not a first-round pick: wide receiver Art Monk, quarterback Jay Schroeder, or wide receiver Michael Westbrook?
6. What NFC West team did the Green Bay Packers defeat 27–17 on the road in the 1995 NFC divisional playoffs?
7. Which one of the following former Houston Oilers draftees was not a first-round pick: safety Blaine Bishop, running back Eddie George, or quarterback Dan Pastorini?
8. By what two-word nickname was Chicago Bears owner George Halas known in his later years with the team?

9. In what year did the Canadian Football League begin play: 1909 or 1959?

10. True or false: Chicago Bears quarterback Erik Kramer played in college at Florida State.

11. What former Minnesota Vikings star was elected to the Minnesota Supreme Court: Jim Marshall, Alan Page, or Ron Yary?

12. Who was the NFL's first African-American coach: Fritz Pollard or Art Shell?

13. What was the nickname of the Buffalo Bills offensive linemen who paved the way for O.J. Simpson's then-record 2,003-yard rushing performance in 1973: "the Electric Company," "Simpson's Stampeders," or "the Steamrollers"?

14. Which one of the following former New York Jets draftees was not a first-round pick: tight end Kyle Brady, running back Blair Thomas, or defensive end Marvin Washington?

15. True or false: Denver Broncos quarterback John Elway never has rushed for at least 100 yards in an NFL game.

16. In 1937 NFL rookie Sammy Baugh signed for the highest salary in league history. What was it: $8,000 or $28,000?

17. What AFC East team did the New England Patriots defeat 31–14 on the road in the 1985 AFC Championship Game?

18. Who is the only player in NFL history to record a run from scrimmage, a reception, and a kickoff return all in excess of 90 yards—and all in the same season: Barry Sanders, Deion Sanders, or Herschel Walker?

19. True or false: Since the AFL-NFL merger in 1970, no defensive player ever has scored a touchdown in three straight games.

20. True or false: Dallas Cowboys fullback Daryl Johnston is a former first-round draft pick.

21. Prior to the 1965 NFL season, officials' penalty flags were not yellow, as they are today. What color were they?

22. What team did the Miami Dolphins defeat 27–24 on a 37-yard Garo Yepremian field goal in overtime on the road in the 1971 AFC divisional playoffs: the Kansas City Chiefs or the San Diego Chargers?

23. Which one of the following former New England Patriots draftees was not a first-round pick: offensive tackle Bruce Armstrong, tight end Ben Coates, or wide receiver Terry Glenn?

24. In addition to football, what sport did Tennessee Oilers wide receiver Chris Sanders star in as a collegian at Ohio State: baseball or track?

25. What position did Hall-of-Famer Bill Dudley—who played for the Pittsburgh Steelers (1942, 1945–46), Detroit Lions (1947–49), and Washington Redskins (1950–51, '53) and went by the nickname "Bullet Bill"—play: end, center, or halfback?

40–49 YARDS
(25 questions)

1. Which NFC West team went 0–4 in 1997 in regular-season games against teams from the AFC: the Atlanta Falcons, Carolina Panthers, or St. Louis Rams?

2. What former Houston Oilers player holds the all-time record (AFL or NFL) for receiving yards by a rookie, with 1,473: Bill Groman, Charley Hennigan, or Haywood Jeffires?

3. What AFC Central team did the Denver Broncos defeat 37–21 at home in the 1989 AFC Championship Game?

4. Who passed Hall-of-Famer Walter Payton in 1996 to set a new NFL career record for rushing touchdowns?

5. Which one of the following former Atlanta Falcons draftees was not a first-round pick: quarterback Steve Bartkowski, quarterback Chris Miller, or defensive end Chuck Smith?

6. What franchise has lost the most NFL championship games, including Super Bowls, with 11 (through the 1997 season): the Buffalo Bills, Dallas Cowboys, or New York Giants?

7. What team did the Miami Dolphins defeat 14–0 at home in the 1982 AFC Championship Game (otherwise known as the "Mud Bowl"): the New York Jets or the Oakland Raiders?

8. Which one of the following former Buffalo Bills draftees was not a first-round pick: quarterback Joe Ferguson, running back O.J. Simpson, or offensive tackle John Fina?

9. What AFL team was embarrassed 38–21 by the Canadian Football League's Hamilton Tigercats in an exhibition game in 1961: the Boston Patriots, Buffalo Bills, or Houston Oilers?

10. What NFC Central rival did the Chicago Bears defeat 35–18 on the road in the 1994 NFC wild-card playoffs in the team's only postseason win under coach Dave Wannstedt (through 1997)?

11. Which one of the following former Cleveland Browns draftees was not a first-round pick: wide receiver Michael Jackson, cornerback Antonio Langham, or tight end Ozzie Newsome?

12. What team did the Philadelphia Eagles defeat 20–7 at home in the 1980 NFC Championship Game: the Chicago Bears or the Dallas Cowboys?

13. What star quarterback of the 1970s first used the term "Hail Mary" to describe a late-game heave to the end zone?

14. Which one of the following former Indianapolis Colts draftees was not a first-round pick: cornerback Ray Buchanan, linebacker Quentin Coryatt, or running back Marshall Faulk?

15. Name the running back who carried for the longest touchdown rush in NFL overtime history, a 60-yarder that gave the Dallas Cowboys a 23–17 victory at the New England Patriots in 1987.

16. What AFC Central team did the Pittsburgh Steelers defeat 26–23 on a Gary Anderson 50-yard field goal in overtime on the road in the 1989 AFC wild-card playoffs?

17. What AFC West team did the Miami Dolphins defeat 31–0 at home in the 1992 AFC divisional playoffs for the only divisional-playoffs shutout in the NFL in the 1990s (through the '97 season)?

18. Name either of the two players whose jersey numbers have been retired by the New Orleans Saints.

19. In what year was the ''in the grasp'' rule—by which officials are instructed to whistle a play dead when a quarterback is clearly in the grasp of a pass-rusher—first instituted by the NFL: 1979, 1986, or 1993?

20. In 1986 NFL owners first adopted instant replay as an officiating aid. Within one either way of the actual number, how many years did the instant-replay system last?

21. Which one of the following former Seattle Seahawks draftees was not a first-round pick: wide receiver Joey Galloway, defensive end Michael Sinclair, or running back Curt Warner?

22. What AFC East team did the San Diego Chargers defeat 41–38 on a Rolf Benirschke 29-yard field goal in overtime on the road in the 1981 AFC divisional playoffs?

23. What NFC West team did the Washington Redskins

defeat 24–21 at home in the 1983 NFC Championship Game?

24. True or false: No player ever has led the NFL in rushing touchdowns and touchdown passes in the same season.

25. What two teams participated in the 1967 NFL title game, otherwise known as the "Ice Bowl"?

50–55 YARDS
(25 questions)

1. What NFC Central team did the San Francisco 49ers defeat 41–13 at home in the 1989 NFC divisional playoffs?

2. What NFC Central team did the Dallas Cowboys defeat 17–13 on the road in the 1991 NFC wild-card playoffs?

3. How wide must the area between the goal posts be: 15 feet (five yards); 18 feet, six inches; 24 feet, six inches; or 30 feet?

4. Which of the following current NFL cornerbacks was a McDonald's All-American basketball player in high school: Ashley Ambrose, Cris Dishman, Walt Harris, or Phillippi Sparks?

5. What AFC East team did the Cleveland Browns defeat 34–30 at home in the 1989 AFC divisional playoffs?

6. What AFC East team did the Houston Oilers defeat 17–10 at home in the 1991 AFC wild-card playoffs?

7. What NFC East team did the Chicago Bears defeat 20–12 at home in the 1988 NFC divisional playoffs?

8. What NFC Central team did the New York Giants defeat 31–3 at home in the 1990 NFC divisional playoffs?

9. Name the only AFC Central team to go a perfect 4–0 in 1997 in regular-season games against teams from the NFC.

10. What NFC West team did the Philadelphia Eagles defeat 36–20 on the road in the 1992 NFC wild-card playoffs?

11. Name the quarterback and wide receiver who hooked up for the longest touchdown pass in NFL overtime history, a 99-yarder that gave the Philadelphia Eagles a 23–17 victory at home over the Atlanta Falcons in 1985.

12. In what facility did the Kansas City Chiefs play their home games from their first year in the city, 1963, through '71?

13. What NFC West team did the Chicago Bears defeat 16–6 at home in the 1990 NFC wild-card playoffs?

14. What AFC West team did the San Diego Chargers defeat 17–0 at home in the 1992 AFC wild-card playoffs?

15. What AFC West team did the Cincinnati Bengals defeat 21–13 at home in the 1988 AFC divisional playoffs?

16. What team did the Jacksonville Jaguars defeat 17–16 on the road in their fifth game of the 1995 season for their first regular-season win ever: the Arizona Cardinals, Dallas Cowboys, Green Bay Packers, or Houston Oilers?

17. Who coached the St. Louis Cardinals from 1973 to 1977: Don Coryell, Bud Grant, Jim Hanifan, or Chuck Noll?

18. Within five either way of the actual number, how many passes did Miami Dolphins quarterback Bob Griese attempt in his team's 24–7 defeat of the Minnesota Vikings in Super Bowl VIII?

19. What AFC Central team did the Cincinnati Bengals

       defeat 41–14 at home in the 1990 AFC wild-card playoffs?

20. What NFL team played in Shibe Park from 1940 to 1957?

21. What NFC West team did the Minnesota Vikings defeat 28–17 at home in the 1988 NFC wild-card playoffs?

22. What AFL team played in Nippert Stadium in 1968 and '69, the first two years of existence for the team?

23. Name either of the two players whose jersey numbers have been retired by the Denver Broncos.

24. What jersey number does Tampa Bay Buccaneers fullback Mike Alstott wear?

25. What was the name of the NFL charter franchise that played in Muncie, Indiana, in 1920 and '21: Flyers, Hoosiers, Marauders, or Warriors?

ANSWERS

Inside the 20

1. Bo Jackson.
2. Steve Largent (number 80).
3. The Indianapolis Colts.
4. Unitas, who wore number 19.
5. Dan Fouts (number 14).
6. "Too Tall."
7. True.
8. Von Oelhoffen, who was selected out of Boise State in the sixth round in 1994.
9. Candlestick Park.
10. False. Irvin played at the University of Miami, where

in three seasons as a starter he set school records for receptions (143), receiving yards (2,423), and touchdown receptions (26).

11. The Detroit Lions.

12. The Green Bay Packers.

13. Number 19.

14. The Orange Bowl.

15. Peyton Manning, a quarterback from Tennessee, who was selected by the Indianapolis Colts.

16. Dallas Cowboys cornerback Deion Sanders, who has played in Super Bowls with the Cowboys and San Francisco 49ers, and played in the World Series with the Atlanta Braves.

17. Cota, who was selected out of the University of Oregon in the seventh round in 1995.

18. Jackie Smith.

19. The San Francisco 49ers, with whom Stubblefield started 75 regular-season games, totaled 39.5 sacks, and played in three Pro Bowls.

20. "White Shoes."

21. Warren Moon, who threw for 33,685 yards and 196 touchdowns with the team from 1984 to 1993.

22. True.

23. Archie Manning, who threw for 21,734 yards and 115 touchdowns with the team from 1971 to 1982.

24. Aska, who was selected out of Central Oklahoma in the third round in 1995.

25. "Hacksaw."

20–29 yards

1. The Cotton Bowl.

2. Lett, who was selected out of Emporia (Kansas) State in the seventh round in 1991.

3. The Chargers, who were 86–48–6 (including their first season, 1960, when the franchise was in Los

Angeles). The Broncos had the worst record of any AFL team: 39–97–4.

4. George Seifert, who took the 49ers job in 1989 and recorded his 100th victory (including playoff games) October 20, 1996, in a 28–21 defeat of the Cincinnati Bengals. The win gave Seifert an overall record of 100–32.

5. It was 1970, the year of the NFL-AFL merger.

6. The Cleveland Browns.

7. Houston, by scores of 34–5 and 27–13, respectively.

8. Lyle, who was selected out of the University of Virginia in the third round in 1994.

9. Number 9.

10. Thirty-five, on five touchdowns and five extra points.

11. Kanell, who was selected out of Florida State in the fourth round in 1996 (but wound up winning the starting quarterback job from Brown the following season, anyway).

12. Jackson State, where he became the NCAA's all-time leader in total points, with 464.

13. The Baltimore Ravens and Philadelphia Eagles tied 10–10 on November 16, and the New York Giants and Washington Redskins tied 7–7 on November 23.

14. False. It's happened once, when the Chicago Bears' David Williams ran one back 95 yards to beat the Detroit Lions 23–17 at Detroit on Thanksgiving Day in 1980.

15. The Vikings, with whom he started 38 games—none in 1990 or '93; he missed both seasons with knee injuries—and rushed for 2,795 yards and 23 touchdowns.

16. Jerry Rice of the San Francisco 49ers. The wide receiver entered the '98 campaign with exactly 1,000 points, on 166 touchdowns and a pair of two-point conversions.

17. The Houston Oilers, then of the AFL, who opened play in the Astrodome in 1968.
18. Texas A&M.
19. Number 93.
20. "Slingin' Sammy" Baugh (number 33).
21. Whelihan, who was selected out of Pacific in the sixth round in 1995.
22. Ken Anderson, who threw for 32,838 yards and 197 touchdowns from 1971 to 1986.
23. Eighty-five, by Tampa Bay Buccaneers running back James Wilder in 1984. For his career, Wilder's 431 receptions included only 10 touchdowns.
24. Ten—all in their 46–10 Super Bowl defeat of the New England Patriots. The Bears beat the Los Angeles Rams 24–0 in the NFC Championship Game after blanking the New York Giants 21–0 in the divisional playoffs.
25. Nine.

30–39 yards

1. True. Allen's rookie season with the Raiders was in 1982, the organization's first year in Los Angeles; he signed as a free agent with the Kansas City Chiefs in '93, two years before the Raiders moved back to Oakland.
2. True. Simpson did it in a 27–14 loss at the Detroit Lions on Thursday, November 25, 1976.
3. The Miami Dolphins.
4. True. Even though the Ravens were only 4–12 in 1996, they went 2–2 against teams from the NFC; in '97, when they were only slightly better overall, they still went 2–1–1 in interconference matchups.
5. Schroeder, who was selected out of UCLA in the third round in 1984.
6. The San Francisco 49ers.

7. Bishop, who was selected out of Ball State in the eighth round in 1993.

8. "Papa Bear."

9. It was 1909.

10. False. Kramer played at North Carolina State, where he broke eight school passing records there and was the Atlantic Coast Conference player of the year as a senior in 1986.

11. Page.

12. Pollard, who co-coached the Akron Pros with Elgie Tobin in 1921 and coached the Hammond (Indiana) Pros alone in '25. The teams' combined record: 8–4–1.

13. "The Electric Company."

14. Washington, who was selected out of the University of Idaho in the sixth round in 1989.

15. True. Elway's career high is 70 yards, set in a 22–21 win at the Oakland Raiders in 1996.

16. It was $8,000.

17. The Miami Dolphins.

18. Walker, who had a 91-yard touchdown run, a 93-yard reception (not for a TD), and a 94-yard kickoff return for a TD as a member of the Philadelphia Eagles in 1994.

19. False. Cornerback Anthony Parker did it as a member of the Minnesota Vikings in 1994, on two interception returns and one fumble return.

20. False. Johnston, who played in college at (and earned a degree in economics from) Syracuse, was selected in the second round (number 39 overall) by the Cowboys in 1989.

21. White.

22. The Kansas City Chiefs.

23. Coates, who was selected out of Livingstone College (which is in Salisbury, North Carolina) in the fifth round in 1991.

24. Track, in which he earned All-America honors in 11 events during his Buckeyes career.
25. Halfback. Dudley's best season was 1946, when he was named the league's most valuable player.

40–49 yards

1. The Rams, who lost at home against the Seattle Seahawks (17–9) and Kansas City Chiefs (28–20), and on the road against the Denver Broncos (35–14) and Oakland Raiders (35–17).
2. Groman, who did it in 1960, the team's first year of existence. Hennigan, who also was a rookie in '60, had 722 receiving yards that season (but went on to best all of Groman's career statistics); Jeffires had only 89 receiving yards as a rookie in '87; and Smith had only 21 receiving yards as a rookie in '80.
3. The Cleveland Browns.
4. Marcus Allen, who passed Payton with his 111th rushing touchdown and finished the 1997 campaign with 123. But the Dallas Cowboys' Emmitt Smith was closing in fast on Allen; he entered the '98 campaign with 112.
5. Smith, who was selected out of the University of Tennessee in the second round in 1992.
6. The New York Giants. The Giants never have lost a Super Bowl, but they've dropped a whopping 11 NFL title games, all from 1933 to 1963.
7. The New York Jets.
8. Ferguson, who was selected out of the University of Nebraska in the third round in 1973.
9. The Buffalo Bills.
10. The Minnesota Vikings.
11. Jackson, who was selected out of Southern Mississippi in the sixth round in 1991.
12. The Dallas Cowboys.
13. Roger Staubach of the Dallas Cowboys.

14. Buchanan, who was selected out of Louisville in the third round in 1993.
15. Herschel Walker.
16. The Houston Oilers.
17. The San Diego Chargers.
18. Jim Taylor (number 31) and Doug Atkins (81).
19. It was 1979.
20. It lasted six years; NFL owners voted the rule down prior to the 1992 season.
21. Sinclair, who was selected out of Eastern New Mexico in the sixth round in 1991.
22. The Miami Dolphins.
23. The San Francisco 49ers.
24. False. Lou "the Hammer" Smyth of the league champion Canton Bulldogs did it in 1923, when he rushed for seven touchdowns and threw for six more.
25. The Green Bay Packers and Dallas Cowboys. At game time in Green Bay, the temperature was 13 degrees below zero, but a brutal wind made conditions feel much worse. The Packers finally won 21–17 on a last-minute quarterback sneak by Bart Starr.

50–55 yards

1. The Minnesota Vikings.
2. The Chicago Bears.
3. Eighteen feet, six inches—precisely the width of the area in between the two sets of hashmarks.
4. Sparks, who averaged 15 points a game as a senior point guard at Maryvale High School in Phoenix.
5. The Buffalo Bills.
6. The New York Jets.
7. The Philadelphia Eagles.
8. The Chicago Bears.
9. The Tennessee Oilers, who won at home against the Washington Redskins (28–14) and New York Giants

(10–6), and on the road against the Arizona Cardinals (41–14) and Dallas Cowboys (27–14).

10. The New Orleans Saints.

11. Ron Jaworski was the quarterback, and Mike Quick was the wide receiver.

12. Municipal Stadium.

13. The New Orleans Saints.

14. The Kansas City Chiefs.

15. The Seattle Seahawks.

16. The Houston Oilers.

17. Coryell, under whom the team was 42–29–1 with two NFC East crowns and earned the nickname "Cardiac Cardinals."

18. Seven, of which Griese completed six for 73 yards— by far all-time Super Bowl lows across the board.

19. The Houston Oilers.

20. The Philadelphia Eagles.

21. The Los Angeles Rams.

22. The Cincinnati Bengals, who moved into Riverfront Stadium (now called Cinergy Field) in 1970.

23. Frank Tripucka (number 18) and Floyd Little (44).

24. Number 40.

25. Flyers.

TWO-POINT CONVERSIONS

(25 questions)

1. True or false: No player ever has passed for 500 or more yards in a "Monday Night Football" game.

2. What jersey number does Kansas City Chiefs quarterback Elvis Grbac wear?

3. Which one of these "Dans" isn't in the Pro Football Hall of Fame: Dan Fouts, Dan Hampton, Dan Dierdorf, or Dan Fortmann?

4. What team did the Minnesota Vikings defeat 36–24 on the road in the 1987 NFC divisional playoffs: the Green Bay Packers or the San Francisco 49ers?

5. True or false: No defensive player has been named NFL most valuable player since Lawrence Taylor in 1986.

6. In what facility did the San Diego Chargers play their home games from 1961 to 1966? (Hint: Sylvester Stallone would have fit in there.)

7. True or false: Former Green Bay Packers coach Vince Lombardi never lost an NFL championship game (including the Super Bowl).

8. Name any two of the four facilities in which the New York Giants played their home games before moving into their current facility in 1976.

9. Who is the only NFL player ever to reach 1,000

yards rushing and 1,000 yards receiving in the same season? (Hint: He accomplished the feat in 1985.)

10. How many games did Hall of Fame running back Jim Brown miss during his nine-year NFL career: none, three, or seven?

11. Since the AFL-NFL merger prior to the 1970 season, what team has the most division titles (through '97), with 16?

12. What jersey number does Minnesota Vikings quarterback Brad Johnson wear?

13. What team did the New England Patriots defeat 27–20 on the road in the 1985 AFC divisional playoffs: the Los Angeles Raiders or the Pittsburgh Steelers?

14. By what nickname was four-time Pro Bowler Carlton Gilchrist—the first 1,000-yard rusher in AFL history—known?

15. Which one of the following former Jacksonville Jaguars draftees was not a first-round pick: defensive end Tony Brackens, linebacker Kevin Hardy, or running back James Stewart?

16. What jersey number does St. Louis Rams quarterback Tony Banks wear?

17. Before a rules change in 1933 made it legal to throw a forward pass from anywhere behind the line of scrimmage, how many yards behind the line of scrimmage did a passer have to be for a forward pass to be legal: five or 10?

18. True or false: Denver Broncos wide receiver Ed McCaffrey played in college at Duke.

19. Within four either way of the actual number, what's the NFL record for most penalties by one team in a single game?

20. True or false: The New England Patriots outgained the Green Bay Packers in total net yardage in Green Bay's 35–21 victory in Super Bowl XXXI.

21. What was the only team ever to beat the Vince Lom-

bardi–coached Green Bay Packers in an NFL championship game: the Cleveland Browns, New York Giants, or Philadelphia Eagles?

22. Within three years either way of the actual answer, before what NFL season were the goalposts moved back 10 yards from the goal line to the end line?

23. True or false: Hall of Fame running back Gale Sayers, whom the Chicago Bears drafted in 1965, also was drafted by an AFL team?

24. Within seven either way of the actual answer, how many players were NFL rosters limited to in 1929?

25. Which one of the following NFLers once played in the Canadian Football League: Antonio Freeman, Kordell Stewart, or Tamarick Vanover?

ANSWERS

1. True. The highest total belongs to former San Francisco 49ers star Joe Montana, who threw for 458 yards in a 30–27 win at the Los Angeles Rams in 1989.

2. Number 18.

3. Hampton, a leader of the great Chicago Bears defenses of the mid- to late-1980s, is not a Hall-of-Famer. Fouts, who passed for 43,040 yards in his San Diego Chargers career, was inducted in 1993; Dierdorf—who was born in Canton, Ohio, site of the Hall—starred at offensive tackle for the St. Louis Cardinals from 1971 through '83 and earned enshrinement in 1996; and the honor came for Fortmann, who was a Chicago Bears starter at the age of 19, in 1965.

4. The San Francisco 49ers.

5. True.
6. Balboa Stadium.
7. False. His teams were 5–1 in title games, the only loss coming by a 17–13 score at the Philadelphia Eagles in 1960.
8. The Polo Grounds (1925–55), Yankee Stadium (1956–73), the Yale Bowl (1973–74), and Shea Stadium (1975).
9. Roger Craig of the San Francisco 49ers, with 1,050 rushing yards and 1,016 receiving yards. It was the only time Craig accomplished the feat in his career.
10. None.
11. The San Francisco 49ers in the NFC West.
12. Number 14.
13. The Los Angeles Raiders.
14. "Cookie."
15. Brackens, who was selected out of the University of Texas in the second round in 1996.
16. Number 12.
17. Five.
18. False. McCaffrey's brother Billy played *basketball* at Duke, but Ed played football at Stanford, where he was All-Pac-10 as a junior and senior, and finished his career with 146 receptions for 2,333 yards and 14 touchdowns.
19. Twenty-two. It's been done twice, most recently by the Chicago Bears in a 1944 game against the Philadelphia Eagles.
20. False. The Packers outgained the Patriots 323 yards to 257.
21. The Eagles, who did it in 1960 with a 17–13 win at home.
22. The 1974 season.
23. True. The Bears outbid the AFL's Kansas City Chiefs for Sayers's services.
24. Eighteen.

25. Vanover, who played for the Las Vegas Posse in 1994 as a wide receiver/kick returner/punt returner before being drafted by the Kansas City Chiefs in '95.

SS. Vegas—who pined for the Las Vegas Class in
buying a wind instrument, he wanted and met
before hours sunset for full initiate. "To Class in
...

STEVE GREENBERG has been a writer and editor for *Inside Sports*, *Football Digest*, *Basketball Digest* and *Hockey Digest* magazines. Currently, he is the managing editor for *Basketball News*, a national weekly magazine. He lives with his wife, Editha, in Chicago.

TEAM UP
WITH FOOTBALL BOOKS
FROM AVON BOOKS

TALKING IRISH:
The Oral History of Notre Dame Football
by Steve Delsohn
97504-1/$24.00 US/$31.00 Can

GREEN BAY REPLAY:
The Packers' Return to Glory
by Dick Schaap
79530-2/$6.99 US/$8.99 Can

THE PRO FOOTBALL TRIVIA BOWL
by Steve Greenberg
79946-4/$5.99 US/$7.99 Can

Compelling True Crime Thrillers
From Avon Books

FATAL PHOTOGRAPHS
by Jack R. Nerad
79770-4/ $6.99 US/ $8.99 Can

CLUB FED
**A TRUE STORY OF LIFE, LIES, AND CRIME
IN THE FEDERAL WITNESS PROTECTION PROGRAM**
by George E. Taylor Jr. with Clifford C. Linedecker
79569-8/ $6.99 US/ $8.99 Can

FATAL MATCH
INSIDE THE MIND OF KILLER MILLIONAIRE JOHN DU PONT
by Bill Ordine and Ralph Vigoda
79105-6/ $6.99 US/ $8.99 Can

SECRETS NEVER LIE
**THE DEATH OF SARA TOKARS—
A SOUTHERN TRAGEDY OF MONEY, MURDER,
AND INNOCENCE BETRAYED**
by Robin McDonald
77752-5/ $6.99 US/ $8.99 Can

THE GOODFELLA TAPES
by George Anastasia
79637-6/ $5.99 US/ $7.99 Can

SPEED KILLS
by Arthur Jay Harris
71932-0/ $5.99 US/ $7.99 Can